Wrestling with Your Destiny

MICHAEL BONORA

DEDICATION

For every hardworking wrestler looking for that extra something, even if you are not sure what that something is.

CONTENTS

ACKNOWLEDGMENTS

First and foremost, I want to thank Alfred C. Martino for helping me understand the publishing process. A special thanks to Lisa Romeo, who improved the manuscript even though she told me she would not. To my family that read the early drafts and made the book you have before you possible. Finally to Christina, who first had to share me with wrestling and then with this book.

PREFACE

This is why you have worked so hard for the past ten years. That was the only thought in my head as I made the walk from the holding area, towards the mat for my championship final. My opponent was shadowing my every move in the opposite corner. Once we stripped off our warm-ups, I heard echoing through the U.S. Cellular Center, "Now wrestling for the 141 pound national title, Michael Bonora, Rhode Island and Jason Adams, Augsburg."

The adrenaline running through my body fueled a nervous excitement, electrifying me even more than the buzz of the packed arena. I was the top seed, undefeated in Division III, wrestling for a school from the smallest state in the nation. My gold singlet shone brightly with the words "Rhode Island College" plastered in maroon across the front.

My opponent was an unseeded sophomore on a run with the tournament's Most Outstanding Wrestler written all over it. If he bested me, the award was sure to be his. The only thing not surprising about his dash to the finals was the powerhouse team he wrestled for. Our paths to the national finals were completely different, but our roads converged on March 8, 2008.

I would be lying if I said my dream was always to be a national champion. Nevertheless, there I was, in Cedar Rapids,

Iowa, with a referee about to signal the start of the final match of my college wrestling career. Seven minutes separated me from my destiny. Then I heard the whistle, my mind went blank and a calm came over me, just as it had hundreds of times before. I was at home for the last time....

I wrote this book because as a young wrestler, I could have used a book like this; to hear from someone who had been through an entire academic wrestling career and could share what he had learned. Throughout my career I often sought out sayings to express how I felt and people to whom I could relate. I always wondered if I was doing everything possible to perform to the best of my ability. Was I thinking the right thoughts, drilling the correct way, lifting the most important muscles? On these pages, I hope I can show you what worked for me and at the very least point you in the right direction.

As you read the following pages remember that this was my journey. The journey an athlete embarks on is an individual one, long and filled with many surprises. The main thing to understand is the uncertainty. Ride the storm out and see where it takes you.

I hope there is something you want from wrestling or athletics in general. If you are unsure, take a moment to think about it. What I set for my own goal is not going to be the same as the goal you set for yourself. Regardless of whether your ambition exceeds mine or not, you can find your own way to be happy with the wrestling chapter of your life. Despite how your last match ends, or even when it occurs, one of the best goals you can set for yourself would be to leave the sport with your head up.

The principles of wrestling can be applied to all aspects of your life to give you that extra edge you need for success. In wrestling and life, a slight advantage can be the difference between achieving your dream or realizing you have to live with your failures.

1

FIRST TASTE

My wild ride to the 2008 National Collegiate Athletic Association (NCAA) Division III Wrestling Championship finals, started when I was in first grade, wrestling in the fifty-five pound weight class. What has stayed with me is how wrestling ended midway through second grade. In the semifinals of a tournament, a fellow second grader lifted my arm and snapped it in two places over his shoulder. My season was instantly over, and so too may have been my whole career.

I decided at the start of third grade that wrestling was not for me. It was not fun anymore. I was only eight, and at that age, if something is not fun, why would any kid want to continue it? This would be the first of two times that I quit wrestling. In hindsight, the broken arm was actually beneficial to my future career. I was not ready to be a wrestler yet. If I had not stopped competing then, I probably would have become burnt out as so many young wrestlers do. They are not competing for enjoyment or the love of the sport, but instead out of habit, family pressure, or to get a scholarship. None of these things are good reasons to stay in any sport.

I loved wrestling, but my desire to train and compete lay dormant for the next five years while I pursued other sports, including soccer and baseball. The yearning to wrestle again was sparked by some unlikely characters. The first was Vince McMahon, who had created the World Wrestling Federation (WWF), now World Wrestling Entertainment (WWE). I watched the WWF on television every week. In the layoff from amateur wrestling, my love for professional wrestling flourished. I idolized charismatic characters such as Hulk Hogan, Bret Hart and others in their company. Even at that young age I already knew that this "professional sport" was scripted. Still, part of me figured the best way to emulate my heroes was to become an amateur wrestler again.

As my love for scholastic wrestling returned after five years, my passion for the WWF waned. I only had room for one kind of wrestling in my life. The wrestling I did was nothing like the pros, although I preferred it for its pureness. Athletics is one of the only true arenas in which greatness can be fairly measured, a rare place where you make your own break instead of waiting for one to miraculously happen.

Another more direct influence on me was my older brother Steve. He started competing in ninth grade for our hometown of Nutley, New Jersey, when I was in the sixth grade and was still watching professional wrestling. He contended in the 171-pound weight class his first season, despite only being 5'2". By his senior season (which was my freshman year), Steve had lost all that pudginess and turned himself into one of the toughest and most exciting wrestlers ever to step foot on a Nutley mat.

Steve and I both have a rare (one in a million) wrist ailment, called Madelung's deformity. It is caused by an extra ligament in our arms. It has twisted our bones to the point where it looks like we have permanent broken wrists. The main obstacle for us to overcome is wrist weakness.

Strong wrists are very useful for wrestlers, because they lead to good grip strength. The more grip strength a wrestler has, the stronger he feels in a clinch. The wrist deformity put us at a disadvantage from the beginning of our careers. Seeing Steve put that aside and successfully wrestle, stoked my interest in the sport, though there was another factor as well.

The final rekindling occurred on my thirteenth birthday, the summer before I entered eighth grade. This was the day a scale rudely informed me that I weighed 137 pounds. I am 5'4" now and just about the only person I am taller than is Steve. I was a fat kid and did not like it. I saw how wrestling had transformed my brother's life and weight, and now I wanted the same. This was almost five and a half years after my broken arm.

From that infamous summer weigh-in when I turned thirteen, until wrestling started that November, I lost twenty-two pounds, mostly through diet rather than exercise. I was not using the highly scrutinized method of weight cutting (taking water out of your body to lower your weight for a short time). Instead, I remember eating cereal for breakfast, lunch and dinner on certain days. Though it was an ill-advised idea because the diet lacked essential nutrients, it proved one thing: I had the discipline to deny myself food, when necessary. That quality allows wrestlers to get to their lowest possible weight, shedding the useless fat on their bodies. However, our bodies need a certain amount of fat to live and function at its highest potential. At that young age I did not know that bit of information.

That first year when I returned to wrestling in the eighth grade, I recall that I was not one of the "good kids." They had been continually wrestling since first grade, unlike myself. They were the ones representing Nutley on the coveted Essex County Team. I, on the other hand, only wrestled in tournaments, which at this age is not as important as the dual meets. You had to make the "County Team," whereas anyone who signed up could enter into tournaments. I used my failure to make the "County Team" as an opportunity to develop my own funky style of wrestling and as motivation to work harder.

I was moderately successful my first season back on the mat. I was largely on my own, learning from watching my brother and other great high school wrestlers. In one match towards the end of the season, my opponent was well above my weight. I lost the match. Nonetheless, my opponent's coach was impressed with the way I wrestled and told me so. His words of encouragement inspired me.

It was the hope of future success which kept me in the sport as a thirteen year old kid.

The groundwork was laid during this year for all the fruits that wrestling would later bear. Besides learning how to be dedicated and determined, it was easy to see how wrestling draws people of all shapes, sizes, and nationalities together, with one thing binding us -- hard work. As teammates push each other, camaraderie develops. Many of my best friends today are those I first made through our mutual participation in wrestling. It may be an individual sport but without good teammates, even the best wrestlers may spoil.

It was sometime after my eighth grade season when I decided I wanted to reach the pinnacle of the New Jersey high school wrestling world. I set the goal to become a state champion by my senior year.

What You Can Take Away from Chapter 1:

1. Figure out what you want from wrestling.

2. Remember that every setback can be useful in some way.

3. Always set high goals for yourself.

2

HIGH SCHOOL

After my goal was in place I knew there was a lot of work to be done before I became a high school wrestler. The goal itself was enough motivation to propel my work ethic to a new level. I decided to join a wrestling club to improve my chances of accomplishing my dream of a state championship. That decision led me to Mike Gibbons, the coach, who educated me with all the basic ingredients I needed to become a successful wrestler. Of all the people who later influenced my wrestling life, Gibbons taught me the most about the physical aspects of the sport during the two years he was my wrestling school instructor. He originally taught me my most effective move, the front headlock.

Gibbons had the most powerful legs which made him extremely difficult to score on. It was a physical attribute I wanted for my own body, and one that I believe is beneficial to all wrestlers. When I think back to the days of wanting stronger legs and a great front headlock, one of the things I remember most is the musky smell of that wrestling room. All wrestlers know this smell. It is a combination of mats, hard work, and sweat, as common to wrestling as the butterflies in one's stomach before each match.

There were two mental strategies that I learned with Gibbons in the first year he was my coach. Mainly, I learned about the nature of dedication. Some nights, there was no one else at the club except for me and Gibbons. He reminded me that, like most wrestling goals, mine was going to take self-motivated dedication

"If your shoulders were on a hot metal plate you would get off your back," Gibbons always said. He made it clear that there was no excuse for getting pinned. The only way it happens is if you give up. It would take me more than hearing those words to learn that. There were other lessons I would learn from Gibbons but we parted ways with the closing of his wrestling school after my freshman year of high school.

My first competition of the ninth grade came in an all freshmen tournament. In the second round at 112 pounds I lost, 10-1. Following the match I was so frustrated, I went for a run outside in the freezing cold for an hour. I somehow thought that subjecting myself to the frigid weather and the tediousness of the run would make me a better wrestler. Just like many who have irrational thoughts after a loss, I obviously did. My reasons for wanting to improve were in the right place even if my methods were not. I wanted to make the varsity team as a freshman and losing to another ninth grader did not help my cause.

The 10-1 loss turned out to be excellent motivation for me. I realized that everyone loses from time to time. Even if I was not the best at that moment, it did not mean I would not end up where I wanted when all was said and done.

My major problem was Nutley's superstar, Anthony Montes, was wrestling at 112 pounds. He was the slickest wrestler I ever wrestled with. During Montes's freshman season (I was in eighth grade) he won districts, took second in the regions and qualified for the state tournament at 103 pounds.

When a kid starts at 103, the idea is to move up one weight class a year to accommodate for growth. This is the exact path Montes took and to me it seemed most great wrestlers did the same. In my freshman year I was very concerned, I could not make the cut from 112 to 103 and the thought of beating Montes at his spot, never entered my mind.

However, the coaching staff noticed something they liked about my wrestling and immediately made Montes my workout partner. Any wrestler knows the importance of a well-matched workout partner and Montes was just that for me at the time. He told me, before big matches, "Just relax and wrestle like you do against me and you'll be fine." This helped tremendously and it is advice I often passed along, while counseling younger teammates.

The most exciting dual meet of my freshman year occurred against our town's rival. As in other big time rivalries it never seemed to matter which team was better on paper. I was on the varsity team at this point and won my match in overtime. The bout of the night was my brother Steve's, when he took on his own personal adversary. Steve used the nervous energy of the crowd to help him and ended up pulling out a 2-1 victory, complete with plenty of drama. His opponent's father was escorted out of the gym by the police. The reason? The referee had not granted his son injury time. Fueled by Steve, our team won the overall dual meet.

After a long struggle my original notion proved true as I was unable to make the lightest weight class in New Jersey high school wrestling. That inability to make 103 or to beat Montes at 112, forced my hand in deciding to challenge Carlos Proano for the 119 pound spot. Carlos and I had already become good friends since he took me under his wing. He was a junior at the time. The whole situation was gut-wrenching for my fourteen year old mind. The coaching staff knew I would garner a better seed at districts and because of that I got the wrestle-off and edged Carlos by a few points. Wrestling is beautiful in that regard, coaches cannot play favorites. The wrestler has to prove his merit and if Carlos had beaten me, he would have gone to districts instead.

In my first District 14 tournament, I entered as the third seed at 119. Up until that point, I had wrestled exclusively at 112.

I had the high point of my season again in a loss. This time, it was a neighboring town's senior star wrestler, who beat me in overtime.

My teammates, parents, coaches and even some guys on other teams told me they were impressed with the way I wrestled. As a freshman receiving all of that praise, my head started to blow up from the attention. My inflated ego was quickly popped in the next match, when I lost again. With a victory, I would have qualified for regions with a chance at making states. Instead, I got cocky, and my season ended right there. I learned never to make that mistake again.

Following the end of my ninth grade season, I knew the two Nutley high school coaches, Carmen Lore and Christopher Chern, were great guys. When I lost in the district wrestlebacks they both voiced words of encouragement to me. It helped me realize that the reason I lost was because I did something wrong, not because I was not good enough. In this case I was overconfident. There is a huge difference between the two trains of thought and yet many people consistently lump them together.

The one thing that sticks out in my mind about Mr. Lore, my head coach, was the saying he told his wrestlers, "You can do anything for six minutes." He always said that before tough matches. This reminded us that the length of a wrestling match is so short that anything is possible, no matter what the odds are. This was a saying I took with me and preached to myself repeatedly throughout my career, especially when I was sick or injured.

Mr. Chern once told me, "I wish we could clone your DNA. Imagine a whole team just like you." That compliment meant so much to me at the time, because he chose to say it, not after I won a big match, but after I lost a heartbreaker. In the years since, it still remains one of the best compliments I have ever received. I am very grateful that both he and Mr. Lore were the coaches during my formative high school years.

For my freshman season I was 9-3 on the varsity level and 17-4 overall, combining varsity, junior varsity, and freshmen matches. I started out 8-0 for varsity. Ironically, that would be my best start to a season and the best team I was part of for years.

It would be in the interim between my freshman and sophomore seasons when I made a decision that would shape so much of my wrestling mentality. I decided to go to the Edge School of Wrestling run by Ernie Monaco, which had a reputation for producing the best wrestlers in New Jersey. I made that choice because I set such high goals for myself.

In our contemporary athletic world, it is almost impossible to attain the highest level of achievement without fully committing to the sport. A high school wrestling season is only four months long, while joining a wrestling school allowed me to practice all year round. I was going to put in the extra work to accomplish my goal. I knew I needed to seek out additional knowledge and that is why I decided to branch out and tap all the resources available to me.

The main thing The Edge taught me was the mental side of being a champion. As I was to learn later, that is more important than the physical aspects of the sport. Club members were told to think and act like champions, even if their skills were not at that level. I also learned to be careful who I compared myself to: To be a state champion, compare yourself to a national champ, not an average wrestler.

Some nights, my dad stayed and watched The Edge classes. On our twenty minute drive back to Nutley, he would ask, "Why did you guys talk most of the night?" My father reasoned that he had paid a good bit of money for me to learn secret moves that could turn opponents into a pretzel. I explained to him that the mental information Ernie gave us was also crucial. The Edge gave me what their name implies -- an edge. I highly recommend wrestlers to go outside of their high school programs as I did. Even without outstanding coaches, a wrestler will improve just by the extra practice.

Coach Monaco also taught me many new moves which I continued to use throughout my career. Three of the most important lessons I learned include, "Fake it, till you make it,"

"Anyone can win when they are up five points. It takes a champion to win when they are down five," and "If your moves would not work on the best in the state, they are not good enough yet."

By the start of my sophomore year, I was ready to use all of the tools I had picked up since my untimely loss the previous season. Unfortunately the story of my sophomore year quickly turned into how to make weight. Since Montes went 119 his junior year, I had to drop back down to 112. I never cut more weight, as I weighed in at 135 in the preseason. This was foolish, of course, because all fifteen year olds are still growing. All I thought and cared about was controlling my food intake, and that severely hindered my wrestling.

This was the only year I dabbled in dangerous weight cutting methods. I thought I had to take water out of my body before every match, using a sauna suit. The sauna suit allowed me to sweat much more rapidly. I also took water pills and exercised and dieted excessively.

The real problem came after I ate dinner. Following some meals, I would run to the bathroom, turn on the shower, so no one would hear, and make myself vomit. I would eat an ice pop after each meal and when I vomited, it would still be cold. This activity itself would probably make a mental health professional classify me as bulimic even though I was not doing it to improve my body image.

I also combined three different weight loss pills on an everyday basis. The worse experience I had all season occurred after I took one of these diet pills. By mistake I ingested it before I had my throw up session. As I threw up, I saw the pill. What I did next still makes me gag. I sifted through my vomit, found the pill, rinsed it off and re-swallowed it. I could have easily taken another. My sick mind clouded my judgment. Everything I did was extremely hazardous and ignorant.

No one knew about these habits since I was good at hiding my activities. One time my mother told me she could not believe parents would let their child cut weight to the point of almost dying. In my head I was thinking, *if you only knew*. What I did was dumb and it really screwed up my body. I threw my metabolism out of whack and I am very lucky I did not do more serious damage.

Even with the boost from The Edge and my own work ethic, I again faltered in key matches. I was eventually able to turn those slipups into learning experiences later on in my career, particularly the weight issues. I learned that an athlete has to improve everyday and any day that does not happen is wasted.

With weight weighing me down, my second high school season of wrestling ended similarly to the first, with an unaccomplished goal. I did not place in the region after finishing second in the districts. When I lost my last match that season I was *happy* because there were no more scales in my near future.

I knew at the time, I still had a lot of work to do to accomplish my ultimate aim of a state championship.

With the conclusion of every match in my career, I always jotted down a little something about it. Below is a partial copy of what I recorded over my sophomore season. I wrote it to reread to myself throughout the year for motivation. Some of the notes were routine, though many reveal key insights from what was going on inside my head at the time.

2000-2001 Wrestling Season (Sophomore)
Goals: Make 112!!!!! At least 25 wins, WIN THE **REGIONS**!! BEAT MARROTA!! GRECO!! Palaez!!
Goals Accomplished: Made 112, Beat Palaez
Goals Not Accomplished: Winning the regions, blew my shot. And every other damn goal.
Overall Record- 24-7
...Dec. 29th, Christmas Tournament
1. WON by fall in 2nd (Pequannock)
2. LOST to Daly 19-9 (Cranford) He took me down 6 times (4 doubles). He put me to my back twice. Other points were 2 escapes. I took around 7 bad shots. Also didn't circle enough.
3. WON 13-5 (PV) Placed third in Tourney
...Feb 2nd, 3rd, **Counties-**
       1st- WON by Pin in First Period. (GR)

2nd- WON by 6 points (Cedar Grove)
3rd- **LOST** in double overtime to Greco
4t- **LOST** to Palaez 1-0 for 3rd place bout.
Placed fourth in Counties- terrible.

...DISTRICTS-
QUARTERFINALS-   WON by Pin in 3rd Period (MKA)
SEMIFINALS-   WON by 3-2 Decision over Palaez
FINALS-   LOST 8-3 to Greco. I wrestled
                     like garbage! Got to use my head!

REGIONS-
PREQUARTERFINALS-   WON by fall in 2nd Period
QUARTERFINALS-   LOST to PV kid that I beat
before, lost 8-7 because I let him reverse me with 5 seconds left.
FIRST ROUND WRESTLEBACKS- LOST to Marrota 15-5,
my year is over.
Season Recap- Did not accomplish main goals. I was not
focused enough at the end of the year. In the quarterfinals of the
regions I really should have beat that PV kid, I beat him earlier in
the year 13-5 but I lost to him when it counts! I need to develop
one more shot. I'll do that over the summer. I did not get pinned
all year, and have not gotten pinned so far in my career. Also I
never lost a home match and hopefully never will. Next year
EVERY GOAL I set will be ACCOMPLISHED.

Reading this summarization now, I realize that I only entered
someone's name when I lost. When I won a match it was not a
big deal. It was what I was supposed to do. The matches that
were the most memorable and important for my growth as a
wrestler were the losses.

After I was eliminated, my mom tried to make me feel
better by telling me, "Those kids who make it to states are a
different breed, they've been wrestling their whole lives."

I nodded, but thought, *next year I will be one of those kids.*
Anything that made me work harder was motivation and in this
instance, my mother's words proved very useful.

Following my sophomore season, my Uncle Lou
explained the importance of jumping rope. It is a secret, boxers

have known for generations, and it was a turning point in my career. Without this advice given and heeded, I would not be retelling my story. Up until that moment, I only had one shot that could consistently take my opponents down; a fireman's carry. That was not enough to reach the high expectations I set for myself. I began jumping rope obsessively in the offseason and because of it became speedy enough for my favorite shot, known as the dart or low single. It is easy to be discouraged by jumping rope. It took me weeks to perform the task correctly and years to perfect it. Keep at it because it will pay off in the end.

In the offseason I had an important decision to make. I had at that time wrestled for three years with my Madelung's deformed wrists. They were progressively becoming worse to the point where the Nutley coaches did not allow me to do any exercise that put unneeded strain on them. Steve had had the surgery to fix one of his arms, after my freshman season, when his wrestling career was over. He told me it helped in the pain department though not in the strength one. It was a scary proposition, to willingly have my arm cut open and my bones and tendons sawed into. However, my left wrist was severally twisted, crooked, and extremely weak. Talking it over with my brother and the rest of my family, I decided to have the operation on my left wrist.

The surgery occurred in March of 2001 and with four months of painful physical therapy, it was apparent the operation was a failure. My left arm became weaker than it already was and two inches shorter than what it was before the surgery. Plus, the pain still nagged me. Naturally, due to the lack of desirable results I decided against attempting the second operation on my right wrist. I resolved that the wrist problems were something I was going to have to deal with for the rest of my life. I told myself many times that they were not to be used as an excuse if I did not accomplish my goal.

After my third year at 112 (eighth grade was really 111) I jumped up to 130 for my junior season. Normally when people make similar leaps in weight it is because they have grown. I, on the contrary, did not grow much in height. I realized that cutting weight was not the way to become a great wrestler. I never again wanted to feel the way I did my sophomore year, when the controlling of food was the most important aspect of my life.

When wrestlers on teams in the surrounding towns learned that I had moved up three classes, they said, "He is too small to wrestle at that weight." I used the doubts as more motivation.

During the year, my workout partner, Montes, brought me to his private coach, Wally. I remembered with Wally, that wrestling did not have to be all work and no play. Having fun is necessary to avoid burnout at all levels of wrestling. Wally, along with my Nutley teammates James Jasnowitz and Ricky Donatiello and others made the grueling sport more enjoyable.

The match in which I learned the most my junior season, had nothing to do with me. It was between Montes and a wrestler from Bergen County, New Jersey. The previous year at states, Montes's counterpart won by technical fall; a loss by fifteen points or more. Despite the lopsided victory, the rematch was highly anticipated all over the state, specifically in the northern parts. More than 1,000 people filled Nutley's gym to capacity.

I was warming up behind the mat, as I was to wrestle immediately following Montes's match. It was one of the rare instances in my career where I put off the warm-up to watch my teammate in action. The match was tied with a minute left in the third and final period. It was a vast improvement for Montes from their previous encounter. In the closing seconds, Montes's legs were tied up in a double leg takedown. As his opponent lifted his legs off the mat to finish the move and win the match, Montes performed a cartwheel to spin out of bounds and get a fresh start. The buzzer rang indicating the end of regulation. In overtime, Montes was the aggressor. He secured a deep single leg takedown and dropped his counterpart for the two points and sudden victory decision.

It was the best match I have ever seen on the high school level. In watching that match, I saw just how powerful the desire to win can be. The match was scheduled specifically for Montes's redemption and he decided there was no way he was going to lose.

Montes carried a 35-0 record into states his senior year. Once there he made the state semifinals before losing three consecutive matches to take sixth. For a long time, I blamed myself because I had failed to give him a planned speech before he left. With time, I came to understand that wrestlers decide their own destiny. If a wrestler is missing tools, mental or physical, it is up to that individual to seek them out. A champion has to be prepared for anything and "leave no stone unturned." I first heard that phrase in 2001 from Wally and it never left me.

My junior season suffered a major setback when I lost in the region quarterfinals after taking second in the district *again*. I wrestled back to take third in the region and technically qualified for states, though I would not actually make it to the NJSIAA Wrestling Championships, which took place in Atlantic City. At the super regions (no longer in existence) I was winning 4-1, before being thrown to my back and losing by two points. This loss should have been enough to make me comprehend the best wrestlers rarely give up back points, especially in the closings seconds of a match. I was not ready to learn that yet. Even with the loss, my sights never deviated from my goal of attaining a state title the following season.

When my junior season was over, I read, *The Oliver Ruiz Story: Something Really Special* written by Jim Maxwell. It is a true story of a wrestler from Cliffside Park, New Jersey, that competed from 1994 to 1998. He had double digit losses on his record and was beaten handily throughout his senior year of high school. In the district finals he was smashed by Dave Cordoba. In the region semis it was Anthony Conte who won by technical fall. Three nights later, he somehow defeated his demons by beating Conte, 4-3, to qualify for the New Jersey state quarterfinals. In his first match at states, he upset the undefeated top seed, before knocking off the once-defeated fourth seed in the semifinals. Now, Ruiz found himself in the state finals against Cordoba, the same guy who had thoroughly stomped him two weeks earlier. However this time, on this day, Ruiz pinned Cordoba at 1:19 into the match to win the 119 pound state title.

I recommend Ruiz's story to anyone. It motivated me through many losses and is proof that anything is possible.

Coach Lore always used to say, "Everybody only has two arms and two legs," meaning any match is winnable. Oliver Ruiz proved that Coach Lore was right.

With the notion that anything was possible, I took my training to a new level. The July before my senior year of high school I worked out at least twice a day. While living at my parent's summer home in Wildwood Crest, NJ, I denied myself many things. When my family went out, I would say, "No, I'm sorry, I have to jump rope," or "I'll meet you there, I'm running." Heading into my senior year, I did not think anyone could have worked harder than me.

The Edge, Mr. Chern and Mr. Lore taught me a lot about the mental side of the sport before this season. In my senior year, I knew I still had to make up for my lack of experience on the mat. That notion led me to Olympic Wrestling Club. It was run by two significant wrestlers, Mike Gibbons, who was previously my coach as a freshman in high school and Florian Ghinea.

A wrestler could not get a better combination of coaches than these two. Gibbons was old school and basic, while Florian was all about crazy moves he was inventing. Gibbons was a NCAA Division I All-American in college while Florian was the youngest ever Romanian National Champion. Florian was also a two-time NCAA Division III champion for Montclair State University.

Florian helped me perfect my fireman's carry, which in turn carried me throughout my career. He improved my front headlock which Gibbons had originally taught me, and The Edge had made better. Florian's final lesson and perhaps most important, was his drag out of a front headlock. This move was instrumental in two of the biggest wins of my career.

When the season commenced a major change for me was in workout partners. Montes had graduated and was replaced with Joe Dwyer. Dwyer brought hard work and dedication to the team every year. He pushed me on the runs and during practice. Hardworking guys are always great to have as teammates, and Dwyer was one of the hardest-working teammates I ever had.

I believed I was going to have a perfect season.

At the first tournament in December, I lost in overtime of the finals. I took an ill-advised shot and my opponent capitalized. A month later I found myself opposite a friend on the Saint Joseph Regional High School wrestling team, Rory O'Donnell. He and I were workout partners at Olympic Wrestling Club.

I was winning 7-2 at the start of the third period. From always practicing with him at Olympic, I knew he had one big move, a headlock. Even with this knowledge I let Rory up to start the third, giving him a free point. I had scored three takedowns already in the match and was confident I could again. Once on our feet Rory hit the headlock to score five points and held me there for the remainder of the match to win by one.

This was the final time I was ever hit with a headlock to my back. It took suffering one of these losses three consecutive years until I learned that particular lesson.

The very next match, I squared off against a great wrestler from the neighboring town of Clifton. I told Mr. Lore to bump me up from my normal weight class of 130, to his weight class of 135. My crushing loss to Rory played into the decision as my pride was getting the best of me. The Clifton wrestler pinned me in thirty seconds and I was as stunned as the Nutley crowd. The loss stayed with me the rest of the year. That was another lesson I still needed to learn -- to let go of losses and focus on the next match, to use previous matches to improve, and not to dwell on past mistakes.

At the start of the district tournament, I was 16-4 and not 35-0, as I had hoped to be. A major factor was electing to take time off during the season for injuries and weight issues. Despite the four losses on my record, remembering Oliver Ruiz kept my confidence to where I believed I was good enough to win states.

With the added help of Gibbons and Florian throughout the year, I was able to beat an old nemesis in the district finals who had bettered me twice my sophomore year. The Star Ledger (Northern New Jersey's major daily newspaper) picked him to win the upcoming regional tournament. Those predictions acted as motivation for me.

I won the Region IV crown by beating him in the finals again. I was now in the company of Nutley wrestling's elite, becoming only its fourth region champion.

One week later was the state tournament in Atlantic City. I won a pre-quarterfinals bout after a first round bye. It set up a match with Jared Mercado the next morning in the state quarterfinals. He was one of the favorites since he had just beaten the defending state champion the weekend before. Our match was 2-1, until the last thirty seconds, when he scored a takedown off a front headlock to increase his lead by two. The takedown deflated me and I was pinned right before time expired.

This loss shattered all my hopes and dreams.

The quarterfinals letdown occurred in March 2003 and for several years I did not think it would ever stop bothering me. In the months that followed my Atlantic City experience, I felt the sport had betrayed me and all my hard work in high school had been wasted. I ended up taking eighth at the state championships and it became a number that I hated to its very core. With the conclusion of the tournament my desire to ever step foot on a mat again vanished.

Here are excerpts from my 2002-2003 senior season notes.

Operation Destination Domination
Goal- STATE TITLE: I FAILED
Record: 23-7 Team record: 9-7-1
January (2003)
...22: Clifton- Got pinned in 30 seconds, I don't know what's wrong with me. Team tied 33-33, but if I didn't get pinned we would have won.
February

...5: <u>Belleville</u>- Teched kid in the 2nd 19-3. Did not wrestle great, I leaned in too much so he hit me with ankle picks but couldn't finish. (I had 4 takedowns) Team lost we def. should have won. Too many kids got pinned, score was 43-27.

8: <u>County Tournament</u>- Did not wrestle- Hip flexor/groin muscle, this was one of the hardest decision I ever had to make to pull out of this tourney my senior year. I decided if I got hurt again I would not be looking too good by district time. So I knew what was more important and I'm trying to keep my eye on the prize.

...22: <u>Randolph</u>- Lost to Kaplan 9-7 and the match was not that close. He bumped up to wrestle me and took me down 4 times, I took him down only once and took so many horrible shots and didn't set anything up. I wrestled really sloppy, I got to fix this before districts. No excuse for this. Team lost 36-33 but if I would've won we would have won.

DISTRICTS: Won Districts...Magic number is now 7.

REGIONS: Won Regions. I'm not wrestling great got to clean up my act by next weekend or I won't be too happy. Magic number is now 4.

STATES: I LOST, MY CAREER IS OVER, I WON THE PREQUARTERS 7-3 OVER PLATT, GOT PINNED IN THE QUARTERS BY MERCADO, BEAT MANCUSO 10-7, LOST TO LIJO 7-4 AND THE LAST MATCH OF MY CAREER LOST TO HELLER 15-8. TOOK 8TH PLACE, HOPEFULLY ONE DAY I WILL SEE THIS AS AN ACCOMPLISHMENT RIGHT NOW IT'S IMPOSSIBLE. I FAILED, I THOUGHT ALL MY HARDWORK WAS GOING TO PAY OFF, I THOUGHT I WAS GOING TO BE A STATE CHAMP. MAYBE IT JUST WASN'T MEANT TO BE. I HAD MY OPPORTUNITIES I JUST DID NOT OR COULD NOT CAPITALIZE ON THEM AND IT COST ME MY DREAM AND IT SUCKS.

<u>Season Recap (Written a week later)</u>

I was meant to be a state champion. All my work was meant to pay off but I did not do it. The reason is because I was afraid to wrestle. Fate took me there like it took Ruiz, I had just as much help, but higher powers cannot win matches for you. Ruiz went out and wasn't afraid to win, he wasn't afraid to try and I was and that is why I am not a state champ. "Fate it only takes you so far, once you're there it's up to you to make it happen." That's a quote I once heard and I think it is one of the truest statements ever made.

When I first wrote this recap, at the age of seventeen, I did not think the words wrestling and future could be used in the same sentence when it came to me. However, five coaches shaped my high school wrestling career both mentally and physically. They gave me all the tools I would need for my future wrestling conquests. Carmen Lore, Chris Chern, Mike Gibbons, Florian Ghinea, and Ernie Monaco, all helped plant a seed in me that would eventually blossom.

What You Can Take Away from Chapter 2:

1. Big time goals take bigger commitments.

2. "Anyone can win when they are up five points. It takes a champion to win when they are down by five."

3. You have to improve every day, either physically or mentally.

4. If you happen to find yourself on the losing end, remember Oliver Ruiz.

3

RECRUITMENT

Following my failure at the state tournament, I had serious doubts about wrestling on the next level. While in high school, the only thing important to me was winning a state title and when that was no longer possible, I did not really care about being a national champion on the collegiate level. That may sound crazy, yet at the time, it was 100 percent true.

After careful consideration between myself and my family, I decided to wrestle. It felt good to be wanted at a college. I always enjoyed when coaches called to check-in on me. Plus, wrestling provided me with built in friends at the college of my choice.

The downside to recruitment is when an athlete is highly desirable. Having a different coach call your house every night can be tedious. Then again, if you do want to compete in college, it is always better to get too many, than too few calls.

During my junior and senior years I was actively recruited by a few different colleges, including two Division I schools -- Wagner College in New York and Franklin and Marshall College in Pennsylvania.

I ruled Wagner out first because it did not feel like a good fit for me. Franklin and Marshall was then dismissed because honestly, after my visit I thought the campus life was lacking. I knew not to make my college decision solely on one factor, whether it be social, academic or athletics. College should be a great place to get a quality education, do what you love, and have fun. All three of those factors affected my decision on which college or university to attend.

The fact that Wagner and Franklin and Marshall competed in Division I, played into my decision as well. Being a Division I athlete is practically a fulltime job. Given my initial doubts about continuing athletics in college, I did not think it would have been a good fit for someone in my mental state. It would have taken a bigger commitment than I was willing to give at the time.

When deciding which students to recruit, college coaches typically look at a wrestler's junior season results. My junior year of high school was a good one. I finished in the top twenty-four in the state of New Jersey, however that was not a result which would attract interest from many Division I programs. There are very few Division II wrestling programs within driving distance of New Jersey and none of them ever contacted me. Consequently, I was most sought after by Division III schools, and participated in overnight visits at Muhlenberg College and Rhode Island College (RIC).

Going to as many recruit nights as possible is good strategy. They are entertaining and give an athlete a chance to get to know the people with whom he or she will be spending massive amounts of time with over the next four or five years.

A lot of coaches had come to the 2003 New Jersey state championships, but only Coach Jones from RIC had made a lasting impression on me. He went out of his way to find me and made me feel like the most important person he had come to see. Throughout my senior year, Coach Jones would always call to check-in and seemed to be a genuinely nice guy.

Rhode Island's recruit night was something different. I went up to see the school with my mom and my Aunt Lorraine.

We went out to eat on Federal Hill, a wonderful Italian section of Providence. Coach Jones set me up with the team's heavyweight wrestler, BJ, and he and Eddy German had the rest of the night planned out for me.

RIC seemed small enough for me to make a name for myself at around 10,000 students. RIC is located in the heart of Providence with eight other colleges in the area. Another plus was that my former teammate, Montes, attended school nearby. In the end, I had to make a decision, and my family and I felt RIC was the best fit for me.

I wrote the following journal pages in the preseason of wrestling, my freshman year at RIC. It reveals how the way a student feels about his high school wrestling career can vastly affect his early college wrestling experience. In this excerpt, I seem almost irrational, and I guess I was then.

11/7/03

Looking back on my career as a Nutley High School wrestler, I realize that all I think about are the bad times. I remember every loss and consider March 15, 2003 the worst day of my life (The day I lost in the state quarterfinals). But now that I'm wrestling in college, I recognize how motivated I really was and how hard I actually did work last year and the years before in my drive to win that state title. It hurts all the time that I didn't win, and I can't ever imagine it going away. I know it's not a big deal to my family or friends but it is to me because I know I did everything I could have to call myself a state champ. Especially last year, I was unbreakable, all the hours running, jumping rope, in the basement shadow drilling, going to The Edge, working with Gibbons/Florian and at NYAC. I thought it was going to pay off, I kept telling myself, when it hurt so much I couldn't even move, that when I won it would be the most blissful thing ever and it would all be worth it. And that moment never came.

It shouldn't have been that important to me, but I made it my life.

Now I see that I wanted the perfect season so bad it paralyzed me. I dreamt about winning every day in school and wrote it on all my notebooks. I thought about what everyone was going to say to me after I won.

If I had gone to states and got destroyed I could have accepted that. But I didn't lose because anyone was better than me or worked harder. I lost the match in my mind.

I did get good out of wrestling. It made me who or what I am. I wonder how I would have turned out, without wrestling. I really don't know. Even though wrestling caused probably more pain than any other thing in my life up to this point, I still am happy I did it. I learned extreme self-discipline and how hard work does pay off—maybe not always in wins, but in other ways. Maybe the greatest lesson I learned from wrestling is: No matter how hard you work, or how bad you want something, sometimes you just don't get it.

I didn't try to wrestleback to take third because to me it was first or nothing. It's not anyone's fault but my own, I blew it and I will have to live with it. I don't care anymore. Wrestling at college was a bad idea, I am not motivated. I am not getting any better, I am not willing to work hard anymore, what should I work for, to take 8th in the state? Screw that.

It's either all the way or nothing, and since right now I don't want to go all the way, it has to be nothing. I can't half-ass this sport. It is 1:35am and I have to be up in five hours for practice. What an idiot I am, I should not be here. Johnny Mariano put it best, when he told me that, I'm just a bitter kid ever since states but that I'm still a champ in his book.... I just wish I was one in mine.

11/8/03

So here is the good I got from this sport, besides the rewards of dedication: Wrestling seriously defined me as a person in a positive way. Without it, I don't think I would have been anywhere near the person I am now, even though right now, I feel like a worthless unmotivated piece of garbage. I think this says it all: Everything I learned in life, everything I know, be it good or bad, I learned and know because of wrestling.

The biggest "good" were the friendships and people I met along the way. I know people from all over the state, and that is a great feeling. Another good is the experience of being "out there" by myself, which is something special. I do have respect for everyone who wrestles; it takes heart.

Anyway winning a match makes me feel superior in some way and I know I'll miss that. I get respect just because I'm good at wrestling. People treat me differently because of it and without that, next year, I'll just be any other kid. Whatever.

What You Can Take Away from Chapter 3:

1. Only wrestle if you want to.

2. If you fail to attain an important goal, try to limit the destructiveness by writing about it or talking to someone you trust.

4

RHODE ISLAND

From the end of March 2003 until September at RIC, I did not step on a wrestling mat. It was the longest layoff of my career and the only year I did not compete in the offseason. I was not motivated and as a result, my development as a wrestler stopped.

My first year as a collegiate athlete was a rollercoaster of emotions. Sometimes I really wanted to wrestle. However, on most days I dreaded the thought. I learned that it is impossible to accomplish great feats when you have no goal. Coach Jones would scream in practice, "Who wants to be a New England champ? Then work hard like one." I would think to myself, "Not me, I want to be a New Jersey state champion."

I was recruited to be a 133-pounder, though the scales never saw that number with me on them. Even with the extra eight pounds, I battled my weight the whole season. I would be nine to ten pounds over, a day before each match. While our other 141-pounder, Luke Emmons, was making the weight, he would often be even heavier than me before a match day. Selfishly, that always made me feel better. Misery likes company.

Making weight was more difficult than it had to be because I was still doing stupid things. I was sucking out water instead of shedding fat, which is exactly what I advise not to do and it hurt me in the long run. On top of that, a college wrestling season is one and half months longer than its high school counterpart. That meant my body had to deal with the extra strain I was needlessly putting on it for a greater period of time.

The first month of college wrestling practice felt like the longest of my life. When the season got underway and I was feeling miserable, I learned a valuable lesson during a conversation with our assistant coach, Bob Smith. The topic turned to my parents worrying about how much weight I had to cut. Coach Smith asked me, "Well, why do they know? What I mean is, why are you really telling them?" While I do not remember my response, his next question was, "Can they run the pounds off for you?" That wise old man made me understand that the only reason I told my parents about the weight cutting was to get some sympathy. I grew up a little after that brief dialogue, and in the years that followed I shared the wisdom I gained with other wrestlers.

My teammates taught me things as well. Whether they intended to or not is a different story. The good times I lacked in wrestling freshman year were alleviated by the friends I made on the team. The guy who sticks most in my mind was Justin Deveau, the big brother of RIC wrestling. He was our captain of captains, our leader and our most valuable wrestler. If I had only followed his example, my freshman year would have undoubtedly turned out better.

At the New England duals, our teamed faced off against Johnson and Wales University (J-Wu). I ended up wrestling my old high school teammate, workout partner and friend, Montes. J-Wu crushed us, 34-9, with Montes downing me, 5-3. It felt very odd to wrestle him. At that time, I was still closer to Montes than anyone on the RIC team. In my head, it was a match I was supposed to lose. He was Montes and I was always going to be in his shadow. After the loss, Coach Smith flatly told me, "You gave him too much respect." I believed Coach Smith and turned those words into the great equalizer: confidence.

Just over two weeks later we had a rematch with J-Wu for the league title. J-Wu bumped up the same guys and Montes and I found ourselves across from each other once again. This time, with Coach Smith's words fresh in my mind, I kept telling myself over the packed gym and screaming fans, "You can do this. You're just as good as him." Towards the end of an action packed scoreless first period, Montes took a shot that I knew was coming. I countered by trapping him in a front headlock. Instead of going for a move he was sure to know, I went for a cement mixer that I rarely ever used and threw him to his back. He rolled through to his stomach surrendering only two points for the takedown. At the end of the first I was up by two. The two point lead remained unchanged when we both escaped from the bottom position to earn one point each in the second and third periods, respectively. However, I had stayed in the top position for a longer amount of time and was only seconds away from eclipsing the one minute mark of riding advantage. If that happened, I earned an extra point. Knowing this and wanting to salt the match away, I shot in. I captured Montes's leg and took him down with a few seconds left to go up by four. The remaining time in the match was enough to earn me the riding point and I won by a final of 6-1.

Our team went on to upset J-Wu, 21-20, to win the match and the Pilgrim League Championship. Eric Martell made one of the most amazing throws I have ever seen to secure the win at 184 pounds. I was elated. It was my first happy moment in wrestling in a long time. In fairness to Montes, he gave up eight pounds to me. That is always a tall order to fill. Montes and I never wrestled one another again. The contest remains my all-time favorite dual match in high school or college.

At the 2004 New England College Conference Wrestling Association (NECCWA, now the easier on the tongue, New England Wrestling Association, NEWA) Championships, I was pinned for the only time in my college career. I distinctly remember a point in the match, which was against Mike Gaeta, when I gave up, as do all wrestlers who wind up getting pinned. Following the match, I thought to myself, "He wanted it more and it showed big time." Gaeta ended up placing fifth at the NCAA Division III championships after winning the New England national qualifier. He would place the next three years as well, to become one of the rare breeds that four-time All-Americans are.

At the end of my freshman season, for the second time in my life I was preparing to walk away from the sport. This time, instead of a broken arm, a fifth place finish at the national qualifier ushered me out. Because I could not motivate myself, I had decided to transfer. Lacking a goal, I did not want to disgrace myself, my school, and the sport.

Here are excerpts from my freshman year recap. Notice the negativity running throughout.

RIC Wrestling 2003-2004 Season [Freshman (and only) Year]

Record= 22-9

...11/22/03: Springfield Tournament- I did not wrestle, I hurt my elbow last weekend and didn't want to attend and be embarrassed. Also my weight was and still is extremely high so I didn't feel like cutting down. Our team placed top 10 without 6 of our starting 10 guys which shows our depth. I'm seriously at a crossroads. I felt bad for not wrestling today and I think I could have won. I really do not know what I want. On the car ride over, I was telling myself I want to win New England's and place in the nation. That would be extremely cool, to be able to call myself an All-American 20 years from now. It is going to take a lot of hard work and I guess I'll just have to wait and see if I can motivate myself. It is already late but I'm going to stop being a baby and give it everything I got one more time.

12/6/03: RIT Tournament- I didn't place. I'm still an unmotivated bastard who can't stop eating, I definitely should be at the least a 133 pound wrestler too bad I don't care enough.

12/11/03: Plymouth State- I pinned him in the 2nd, but I was losing 8-5 at the time. I was wrestling like garbage, too slow and couldn't move. I have to lose weight the right way. Anyway, I was losing, when the kid took a bad shot I caught and pinned him. Place went nuts, it was cool. I'm now 8-3 and done with wrestling until Jan. 4. Team is 1-0.

12/29-30: Citrus Invitational: I'm not going to Florida over Christmas break. I'll be home wrestling with my high school team and eating some good food.

1/04/04: Simpson (Iowa), Williams, Norwich: I lost to the damn Simpson kid 7-6 cause I blow and can't stall. With 20 seconds left, got taken down to lose. Didn't wrestle well against the Williams kid but still won, and I beat Conklin from Norwich pretty good, he was ranked 4th in New England and I'm ranked 2nd. Somehow he was ranked 8th in the country...not anymore. So I kept my ranking at least. I beat Foresi who was ranked 6th in the country and Conklin who was ranked 8th. I bet I could win this whole thing if I cared but I don't and I won't. Team barely beat Williams, got killed by the Iowa team and Lost 20-13 to Norwich.

...1/21/04: WPI: I won 20-7. Team lost 25-19 to the 28th ranked team in the country. We could have won but oh well. A month from today the season is over haha yeah.

2/14/04: I bumped up to 149 to wrestle some Bridgewater kid. I won 10-4 because I got reversed with 10 seconds left but whatever it's alright a win is a win. If this is going to be my last year, that was the last dual match of my career.

New England's- Placed 5th, Pinned some kid 1st, then beat Bucco form Norwich, then lost to Fierro-Fine 5-4, then got killed by Gaeta, he just kept putting me to my back, then beat the WPI kid 7-4 for 5th. It was the last match of my life, I am pretty sure. Thanks WRESTLING.

What You Can Take Away from Chapter 4:

1. Looking for sympathy will get you nowhere.

2. You can reverse negative outcomes to your favor in a very short time.

3. One step back may be the only way forward.

5

HOFSTRA

I transferred to Hofstra University in Hempstead, New York following my freshman year at RIC. The decision was made because two of my good friends were at Hofstra. In the back of my mind, and in all likelihood maybe the real reason on a subconscious level, I knew they had a Division I wrestling team. I thought if I ever decided I wanted to wrestle again, I would not have to transfer for a second time.

An NCAA rule mandates that any transfer from a Division III institution has to sit out one year before they are eligible to compete at the Division I level. The reason behind that rule is that it keeps Division III more competitive. Either way, this rule did not pertain to me. I had no plans of wrestling.

During transfer orientation I learned something that would prove fundamental down the road. Similar to most things in life, I did not realize it at the time. I was asked how well I knew the Spanish language. I had taken four years of Spanish in high school, but I told the questioner, "I don't know anything. I should be in a level one class."

His response was, "How could you let them do that to you? Four years and you don't think you learned anything?"

I stared at him blankly. Now, I comprehend the point he was trying to make. In my high school Spanish classes, I had been in a situation where I was not learning. It was my job to get out of it or to make the most of it. I never did and all of the time was wasted. The lesson was transferable to wrestling, I would later realize, and to many other situations as well.

The first semester at Hofstra, in the fall of 2004, wrestling did not cross my mind. I needed a mental break and that was exactly what I got. It was nice to be free of the 24/7, all-consuming wrestling thoughts. That spring, the first inklings of change sprung at me as I made my way to watch the last match of the Hofstra wrestling season. Coincidently, it happened to be senior night for the Hofstra team. Two seniors were honored that night, both former New Jersey state champions, Chris Skretkowicz and Ricky Laforge.

After the Hofstra team's wrestling season ended, I started to feel the itch to get back on the mat. I contacted Tom Ryan, Hofstra's head coach at the time. He invited me to open mats the very next day. As the open mat session was concluding, Coach Ryan was watching me going at it with one of his starters. He called me over and said, "I want you on my team." Then he asked, "Were you the hardest working guy on your team in high school?" I hesitated and said yes. He nodded and smiled. I continued to workout with Hofstra until the end of the semester with plans of joining them at the start of the 2005-2006 season.

Before that could come to fruition, I contracted mononucleosis and it foiled my plans for a return to wrestling. I was forced to discontinue working out for more than a month. I lost all the progress I had made and needed another few months just to get back to where I was before the illness. A Hofstra assistant coach called at the end of the summer to tell me team workouts would begin the same day school started. The month in bed battling mono had given me mixed feelings again about wrestling, and I declined his offer. I did not think I was ready to start practicing with a top Division I team. I told myself to forget wrestling and move on.

That proved to be impossible.

Mike Riley, a wrestler from the Rhode Island area, was a key to my return. We were talking online sometime during the early part of my third semester at Hofstra, in the fall of 2005. I told him I was not sure what to do. He replied, "Stop being a baby about this decision, make one and stick to it. Stop saying you are probably going to do one thing or the other." I did not know how to respond and remember being pretty mad at the time. What he said made me stop and think about what I really wanted to do. It ultimately helped me decide I could not put my passion for the sport off any longer. I realized I would have my whole life after wrestling to enjoy the parties, food, and relaxing days that most people take for granted. There is only a limited amount of time to be a college athlete. The realization was ironic since many other people had already voiced similar notions without it ever sinking in.

The Hofstra team had been training since the end of the previous season, and I was just starting to get back into it. I wanted to be one of the ten starters in the second semester. To be honest, at the Division I level, I did not think it was possible. Luckily, I had another option. Coach Jones had kept in contact and let me know the RIC door was still open.

I remember the exact moment I decided to transfer back to RIC. I was at Penn State visiting my girlfriend, Christina. We were in the mall when a former teammate, Matt Kelly, called me on my cell phone. He had heard that I was thinking of coming back and told me he had an open room for the start of the second semester. Without anymore thought I told him, "I'll take it," and I became one of the boys of 50 Gloucester, by moving to that street address in Providence. I had been unsure of what to do and this call was the sign that made it clear to me. I was a wrestler who belonged at RIC and I could not run from that any longer.

What You Can Take Away from Chapter 5:

1. A mental break can be very refreshing, energizing, and positive.

2. Do not run from what you are.

3. You will know what to do when the time comes.

6

REFRESHED

During my abbreviated sophomore season of eligibility, I was finally able to get over my shattered dream of not having won a New Jersey state championship. The absence from the sport refreshed my love for it. I had a new goal -- to become a Division III national champion. In my first season back on the mat, I assumed that goal would be a stretch. By this time, I had not wrestled competitively in almost two years.

At my opening competition of the season, I was watching Luis Felix, our 157 pound wrestler for the first time, when he was taken down to his back. Felix was looking directly at our bench as we screamed at him to get off his back. He just smiled and kept chewing his gum, as if he did not have a care in the world. Twenty seconds later he flipped his opponent over and stuck him for the fall.

The night before the New England duals, one of my new teammates, Nick, went to another team member's house and took the team scale. Since no one was home, Nick decided to write a note explaining he had the scale, a commendable thing to do. The note said in effect, that he was having weight issues and needed the scale to make sure he was on weight in the morning. The only problem was he decided to write this note on the front door, with a permanent marker.

As we were getting skin checked for the tournament the following day, Nick told Coach Jones he was overweight.

Coach asked, "How much? Half a pound?"

Nick moved his head slowly left to right and responded, "four."

"Four tenths is nothing Nick," Coach Jones replied. "Start running."

"No," Nick said. "I'm four *pounds* over."

Our captain at the time, Todd Bloom, said with an expressionless face, "Well Nick, did you check all the scales?"

During any wrestling season many funny moments happen and this proved true again. Even though wrestling is such a serious sport, many good times come from it. I learned in high school that if you never have any fun, you will not last long as a serious athlete. The funny moments usually center around your teammates.

After Nick's weight fiasco, I beat the second ranked New England wrestler, Andrew Lacroix. In our rematch the following week, he bounced back, blemishing my 10-0 record. I lost because he turned me to my back and that was always very hard for me to accept.

I went into the NECCWA Championships as the three seed with a record of 14-1. It set up a third match with Lacroix in the semifinals, the biggest stage of my season, where I faltered yet again. This time I remembered past lessons, and I looked for good in the situation. I noticed something valuable from the loss. I was getting in on my shots with ease but could not finish them. I came to the realization that this was because I rarely finished my shots to the mat in practice. I made it my mission to drill my moves all the way the following season to correct the glitch in my wrestling.

Despite the loss in the semifinals, the way the New England brackets are set up, I was still alive to win the tournament.

In a match to see who would wrestle the loser of the first finals, I faced Mike Conklin. He was a wrestler whom I had beaten as a freshman by eight points and I completely looked passed him to my potential rematch with Lacroix. The match started with Conklin catching me off guard and taking me down with a double leg. I fought my way back and did not mentally count myself out. With thirty seconds left, the match was tied. I took a shot, got in and hesitated *again*. He had enough time to react and get behind me for the takedown. My season was over with a fourth place finish at the conference championships. Gaeta ended up losing to Lacroix in the first finals, but then came back to beat Conklin and Lacroix twice, for his third New England title in as many years.

As I had done during all my previous seasons, I wrote a match by match summary. As I re-read it, I noticed the only lesson to take away was putting the responsibility of losing on your own shoulders. I gave wrestlers credit for beating me but I knew that every match I lost, had been winnable. If I had written "I lost to a better wrestler and there was nothing I could do," then guess what, I would never beat that guy. I realized that when I lost a match there was a reason for it, regardless of the score, and if I could correct my mistakes, I would win next time.

After that season one of our assistant coaches, Scott Baum, made his departure from the team. What I admired about Coach Baum was his honesty. He often told us, "I was not the best wrestler, but I worked as hard as I could and made the most of my God given talents." That is what he expected of us and that is what I strove to do.

What You Can Take Away from Chapter 6:

1. Never overlook anyone as every opponent is dangerous and can beat you on any day.

2. Take responsibility for your losses. Figure out what went wrong and fix it.

3. Drill your moves to the mat more often than not.

7

BREAKTHROUGH

I had learned the benefit of offseason work even before high school. During spring, following my sophomore season, I competed in a series of open tournaments. For the first time in my career, I won a competition without being the top seed. It was an important step for my confidence.

Sometime in the summer before my junior year, Coach Jones asked me to cut down a weight class, which would have greatly increased my probability of getting to nationals the following year. I gave his recommendation serious thought. I reassessed myself and decided I had two major problems: I could not finish my takedowns on high caliber guys and I was too weak to be in 141 pound weight class. In the end I decided not to run from anyone and added ten pounds of muscle by putting in lots of time at the gym. On top of that, every time I drilled, I finished the takedowns to the mat.

"Never run, never scared." Living that motto is much more difficult than saying it. I found that by forcing myself never to run from anyone, never being scared would happen on its own.

To get out of New England and make it to nationals was going to be a monumental task my junior year. In the preseason National Wrestling Coaches Association (NWCA) poll, the three guys ranked ahead of me in New England were ranked one, three and seven in the country.

In addition to my nationally ranked opponents, John Marsh transferred to Bridgewater State College in Massachusetts from Slippery Rock. J-Wu had Steve Eberle, who would be a significant opponent for me. The 141 pound weight class in 2006-07 was shaping up to be the toughest in New England history. Nevertheless, it was there where I made my stand. In my mind, I was going to go undefeated, win a Division III national title and ride off into the sunset. No one thought I could, and that was motivating. I knew the best everyone hoped for me was to take third in the qualifier and just manage to get to nationals. I held myself to a higher standard.

If I could win nationals in my junior year, I would leave RIC following the spring 2007 semester. I was graduating in May regardless of how wrestling panned out. I also wanted to break the single season win and takedown records at my school. The win record was forty-one and to better it I would not be able to sit out of many matches. This proved to be a very significant piece of the puzzle for me.

I was more focused than I had ever been. I knew what I wanted and what it was going to take to get there. I wanted a national title, although I knew I had to focus on the New England tournament first. If I had a bad tournament in late February, I would not even be making the trip to Iowa where the NCAA championships were held.

I started the year under the national radar. The New England conference is one of the weakest of the nine regions that make up the Division III tournament. The conference had not had a national champion since 1994 when RIC's only champ, Billy Cotter, won at 134 pounds. In fact, New England only had two national collegiate champions in its history.

The season was hands down the most fun I ever had because the guys on the team were friends first and teammates second. No one expected anything from us and I only had my self-imposed pressure. It was the one time in my career I did not have a countdown until the end of the season.

The beginning of the year both of Coach Jones's assistants (Baum and Smith) had quit for different reasons. RIC wrestling had two new assistant coaches, former teammates of mine, Keith Nelson and Dave Paquette. While they lacked the seasoned experience of weathered coaches, they brought new dynamics to the team. The way it turned out, Keith ran practice. Jones and Paquette jumped in from time to time and also dealt with the athletic director, recruiting, and planning trips.

Todd Bloom was a part of this team too, as a student volunteer assistant. All volunteer coaches should be commended. The amount of time invested is tremendous and to receive no monetary payment seems unfair. Todd was one of those guys who, if our paths had not crossed, I would not have had as many successes.

Besides the adjustment of having new assistant coaches, this year of RIC wrestling had a few other problems. They included being captainless for a good part of the season, headgear disputes, and drilling and sprinting issues. The situations were not handled well on the team's nor the coaches' sides. Yet a great thing emerged from the chaos; the athletes on our team grew even closer to one another.

During our inter-squad match in the preseason, Team Gold, which happened to by my side, had the mock dual won heading into the final match. Our starting heavyweight, Andrew Algarin was on my team and almost a sure win for us. Algarin and Sean Miele, the other 141, devised a ploy. During his match, Algarin had built a sizable lead, and then he screamed, fell down and feigned an injury. The trainer rushed onto the mat. Algarin made the injury time sign and Miele threw him a Snickers bar. He took a bite and starting running around like the energizer bunny. When the match resumed, he pinned our other heavyweight putting an exclamation point on the fun mock dual meet.

Even after the first month of the season, which began like a hurricane, I knew the waters would calm and I expected to get off to a good start. To my chagrin, it did not turn out that way. In my second match at the Roger Williams Invitational I lost in the quarterfinals to Steve Eberle from J-Wu. I had beaten him twice the year before. I began to seriously doubt myself and sent my younger brother Robbie this text message, "Maybe I'm just not as good as I think."

I had to wrestle four more matches to take third, beating Eberle in the consolation finals. I was not happy but was somewhat satisfied that I was able to wrestleback. I knew that if you lose a match in the New England tournament you can still wrestleback to win. Wrestling back was something I had not done well in the past. My spirits were also kept up by the knowledge that the very next weekend I would have another crack at many of the same opponents.

In the semifinals of the tournament hosted by Springfield College the following weekend, I ended up wrestling Lacroix, the nation's top ranked wrestler. The result was the same as our previous two matches, a decision loss. I was livid and foolishly kicked a wall, injuring my foot, which bothered me for around three weeks.

Although I did not know it at the time, this cloud had a silver lining. I saw that I had to take the match out of the official's hands and "widen the gap" between myself and my opponents. In particular I learned how to score from the neutral position with my reverse leg wrapped around my opponent's near leg. With the lessons learned, I rebounded to take third. This time I was not even slightly content.

Two weeks later I had another huge tournament in Rochester, New York. I got the number two seed, with Paul LeBlanc, the fourth place finisher at the 2006 NCAAs, as the number one. In the semifinals, I lost by a point in the closing seconds to a different wrestler from Case Western Reserve. It was a crushing defeat. Not only did I lose in all three of the first competitions of the season, but the wrestlers who beat me did not even go on to win those tournaments.

At this point, I had not been in a finals since the first competition of my freshman year.

I walked off the mat and slumped against the wall with my chin down. Coach Jones found me, put his hand on my head and urged me to wrestleback and take third because, "something like this might happen at New England's." It was good to hear those encouraging words. I did wrestleback to take third, after I got a few quick stitches to fix a gash over my eye.

Losses can help you realize you need help. This particular loss made me work very hard to correct my weaknesses in the practice room. The setback dropped my record to 14-3 on the year. I then went on a thirty plus match winning streak, the longest of my career. I allowed myself to be happy for minutes after each win and then I started to focus on the next match. Winning more than thirty consecutive matches was a big step in the right direction but it was never my goal. The goal was to win a New England title, and then hopefully, a national one. I learned to never enjoy a semifinals win too much, as it might take my eyes off the true goal of winning the finals.

During the winning streak, I won my first ever NCAA sanctioned tournament, the Citrus Invitational in Fort Lauderdale, Florida. Going away as a team strengthened our friendships and we grew even closer than we already were.

During one of the matches at the tournament, our 133 pound wrestler, Ray Hanley, saw our 165, Arty Privedenyuk, scanning the crowd before his match. Ray asked Arty what he was looking for. Arty responded, "Motivation. I wrestle better in front of beautiful girls."

The New England duals hosted by Bridgewater State College was my next match of note. Our first round opponents were Norwich University, Mike Conklin's team. He was ranked fourth in the nation at the time. The morning of the match Coach Jones asked me if I wanted to wrestle him. I thought about what I had told myself at the beginning of the season: "Never run, never scared." I also thought about how he ended my season the previous year and wanted to right that wrong.

In the eyes of the New England faithful I was the underdog. But I was confident I would prevail if I wrestled smartly by keeping the match on our feet, in my best position.

Right away I slipped up when he took me down and I landed on my back for two seconds. I found myself in a four point hole. My teammates were super supportive during the back-and-forth bout and I never gave up. I escaped and went on to take him down five times to win by a final of 12-10. My teammates were going nuts when the buzzer sounded and it was one of those moments that make all the hard work worth it.

The bout of the afternoon was not mine and Conklin's, but that of one of my best friends, Ray. He was pitted against the number two ranked wrestler in the nation, who had beaten him three times already. However in this match, Ray secured a fall from the top position as he had done to so many other opponents. No matter the odds, anything is possible in a wrestling match.

After the New England duals, I was ranked sixth in the nation. A teammate congratulated me by saying, "It means nothing but it's still cool." To me it *did* have meaning. It meant that other people now saw something in me, which I knew was there all along. I was no longer just a good wrestler. For the first time, I was a nationally ranked one.

Before the conference championships I was having a conversation with former teammate, Luis Felix, about my weight class. "That weight is like four lions (Gaeta, Conklin, Lacroix and me) going at it," he said. "I can't wait to see it."

I responded with, "yeah," however in my head I told myself, "They may be lions, but I'm a shark and we're in water."

Heading into the national qualifier in February, the way the seeds were going to be awarded was up in the air. At the time Gaeta was ranked fourth in the country, I was fifth, and Conklin dropped to sixth after I beat him. Lacroix was no longer ranked but had beaten me the only time we wrestled in November, and to his credit he placed third in the country the previous year. I had not lost a match in nearly three months, yet somehow the fourth seed had my name behind it. That meant I had to wrestle, three-time defending New England champion, Gaeta, in the semifinals.

Ray told me, "Those damn coaches disrespected you and you better take it out on everyone." The fourth seed, along with Ray's words gave me extra motivation. I text messaged Robbie about my seed and he responded, "It doesn't matter when you wrestle Gaeta because you're winning it."

The seeds also set up a familiar situation. It put me against the fifth seed, Eberle, in the quarterfinals. That was the same scenario as the beginning of the year when I lost at the Roger Williams tournament. Ironically, the New England championships were hosted by Roger Williams that season.

I was confident I could beat Lacroix and Conklin, but Gaeta was a question mark. The last time we were on a mat together was during my freshman year when he pinned me in a match that was not even close. I wanted "it" much more this time around and that was comforting. All I could do was take it one match at a time.

Some wrestlers do not like to look at the bracket. They say it influences their wrestling. I personally want to know the path I must travel to win. I liked to study my opponent to figure out his weaknesses and attack them. I equate not knowing who you are wrestling, to entering into a war without any knowledge of the country you will be fighting.

When the 2007 New England championships got underway I did not make the same mistake I made at the Roger Williams tournament. I handled Eberle in the quarterfinals after a first round bye. Gaeta also did his job to set up our semifinals showdown. On the other hand, the bottom half of the bracket was not going according to plan. Conklin was upset by John Marsh in the quarterfinals. In his semifinals, Marsh's sensational run continued as he pinned Lacroix. This guaranteed him, at worst, a third place finish. Meaning that, Lacroix, Conklin, or whoever lost in my match against Gaeta would take fifth and not make it to nationals. The New England coaches would never give one of their four wild cards to a fifth place finisher.

I reviewed the previous lessons that I had written down throughout my career. The price of the lessons were high, but now I planned on cashing them in.

The whistle blew and Gaeta and I were both very active in our attempts to score first. Shots and counters were followed by more shots and counters. Neither of us could gain the upper hand as we flowed from move to move. Gaeta then took a half shot that fooled me. That gave him enough time to hit the move he intended to all along, a duck-under. I turned to face him as fast as I could and he transitioned to a high single leg. I dropped to one knee and fought him off as his arms reached across to my far ankle in an attempt to get the first two points. I was able to roll both of our bodies out of bounds and get a fresh start. Right when the match recommenced, I faked a high crotch to one leg and went for a low single on the other. It caught Gaeta completely off guard. When my shoulder rammed into his shin, his leg buckled and he fell down, earning me the takedown. He quickly escaped making the score 2-1 at the end of the first.

I chose down to start the second period and escaped in less than fifteen seconds to increase my lead to two. On our feet was where this match was going to be won. I went for my most effective shot, a fireman's carry. I captured Gaeta's leg and threw him over my head. He was able to get to his hips and stop me from earning the takedown. With a lot more action but no scoring, the second period ended with me up 3-1.

Gaeta chose down in the final period and escaped very quickly, again, cutting my lead to one. In my head I told myself, "one more takedown and this match is mine." I shot in and got trapped in a front headlock. Without thinking I slipped my arms around Gaeta's back dropping him to his stomach and scoring two more points. It was an arm drag finish that Florian had taught me years earlier. I breathed a sigh of relief, but Gaeta did not let me enjoy the moment. He escaped and took me down with a high single to tie the match at five. There were twenty seconds left on the clock. If he held me down for the final seconds we would move to overtime. I fought to my base, then to my feet and broke away from his grip earning me the point I needed to win the match. It was the biggest victory of my career and after I shook hands with Gaeta, I walked off the mat and wrapped Robbie in a big hug.

What You Can Take Away from Chapter 7:

1. Rankings should make you work harder, whether you are number one or one hundred.

2. "Never run, never scared."

3. Take it one match at a time.

4. Hard work in the offseason is when you make the most gains.

5. To be the best, you have to beat the best.

8

RELIEF

The most interesting part of the 2007 NECCWA Championships for me, occurred after the semifinals, when I saw Gaeta in the locker room. We had never had a conversation before and at that moment no one else was around. I attempted to lighten the awkward moment with a joke. He acknowledged it with a faint smile and expressed his doubts about making it to nationals his final year. On Sunday morning he had to wrestle a gauntlet of nationally ranked wrestlers. If I had not worked so hard to get where I was, I would have felt bad for him.

I said, "We both know I'm going to be wrestling you tomorrow night in the finals."

"Yeah, I don't know," he responded.

I countered with, "I do," and walked away. I do not know if that brief conversation helped him but I like to think that it did. Why I said that to a future opponent, I cannot say for sure. I guess I could feel his pain. Or maybe it was because Gaeta brought out the best wrestling in me. I owed him for that. Either way, if I was going to win I wanted to beat the best at his best.

Number one seeds are only that way because they beat the best, when they themselves were the underdog.

In the morning, I was to face Marsh. I had beaten him by twelve points a week before. Instead of being overconfident, I thought about Oliver Ruiz and how the score of our previous meetings meant nothing. Nobody rolled over at this level.

During our first finals match the next morning, I quickly saw Marsh was on top of his game. I was having trouble securing takedowns, which came easily the last time we met. I squeaked out a one point win. The victory pretty much guaranteed my ticket to Iowa.

The winner of the first finals got to rest and wait to see whom they would wrestle in the second finals. I mentally prepared for Gaeta. No matter what happens during the season, the defending champions almost always are around in the end. Champions have that ability to perform when it counts most. I knew Gaeta had it and I knew it would be him, in spite of the tough road he had to travel that morning.

At the conference championships, due to the urging of my teammate, Mike Martini, I took naps. There was over five hours between my matches. The naps reenergized me and kept my mind from over thinking what I had to do. My father always told me, "It takes a full two hours to completely wake up." Whether true or not, I made sure I was awake at least two hours before my next scheduled match.

While I was resting, Gaeta beat Conklin, Lacroix, and Marsh to make it back to the finals for a fourth straight year. Only I was left standing in his way. My win in the semifinals gave me a distinct advantage; for him to be crowned the champ, he had to beat me twice. Lingering in my mind was the fact that he had done it the previous year to Lacroix.

When the final match came around, I was just as nervous as I was before every other match of my career. I was riding a huge winning streak and made it to my first-ever conference finals. He had the experience and I countered that with a hunger to be number one. The lights were dimmed and a spotlight was hanging over the mat reminiscent of my high school wrestling days. All the seats in the small gym were filled with screaming fans.

The bout started with a takedown by me followed by a quick escape from Gaeta. Then the previous encounters were flip-flopped to knot the match at three. We both scored a point from bottom when we chose down. We found ourselves tied at four with a minute left. I took a shot on the edge of the mat and got behind him for a split second before we scrambled out of bounds. I hoped for the two points but was not awarded them. Many of the RIC fans were booing, while the side referee conferred with the head official. The call was reversed. Now it was the Springfield fans' turn to go nuts. There were around thirty seconds left. Gaeta escaped to make it, 6-5, took a great shot, and got my left leg in the air. I momentarily thought, "not good," but did not have time to think anything else. I was able to slip my leg out and hold on for the win.

I was the 2007, 141 pound, New England Champion.

It was as if the weight of the world had been lifted off my shoulders. My teammate, Nick Logan, nailed it on the head when he said, "It was pure relief and not happiness I saw on your face after the match." In truth I was both relieved *and* happy, but definitely more relieved.

Gaeta, Marsh, and Lacroix were given three of the four New England wild card bids to nationals. Conklin was the odd man out, which was a shame. He had dominated a wrestler who would earn All-American status two weeks later. The whole weight class was unpredictable, with the wrestler who took third in the country the previous season, taking fourth in the conference championships.

The sense of accomplishment I felt when I was on top of the New England podium was a feeling I had never experienced before. I felt as if I had conquered the world, when no one thought I could. When I look back on those pictures from that night, the smile on my face can still produce the same reaction today.

My parents, Robbie, and I went out to eat after the tournament. Strangely, I felt there was something missing (besides my older brother Steve). To this day I am not exactly sure what it was. They kept asking, "Why aren't you happier?" I guess it was a letdown to be done, after I had worked so hard to accomplish that goal.

In between this tournament and the NCAAs, Martini, Miele, and Ray worked out with me almost every day. It was probably not an ideal day for wrestlers whose seasons had just ended, and I greatly appreciate what the three of them did for me.

During the off weekend between the two tournaments, I decided to go home to New Jersey for the first time in over three months. I thought it would be a good mental break.

Coach Jones and I flew to Cedar Rapids, Iowa, the Wednesday before the competition. Then we made the one hour drive to Dubuque, where the 2007 NCAA Division III championships were held. Prior to the flight, my girlfriend- Christina had advised me to watch some funny movies. "Laughter is good for you," she had said. I agreed and practiced what she preached.

It was a magnificent feeling arriving at the workout facility in Dubuque and receiving the qualification gift (an NCAA cooler on wheels). With the registration process complete, I stepped onto the mats and looked around. I knew then I had accomplished something and had made it to "the dance." In one of my favorite songs, the band Bad Religion sings, "What good is skill if you don't make it to the dance? Despite circumstance, you've got a chance."

After a quick workout, we checked into our hotel. When I was unpacking, I looked down to see two coloring books among my belongings, and smiled. Going back to this childhood activity calmed me down when I was nervous. The idiosyncrasy did not embarrass me and everyone got a good laugh at a twenty-one year old New England champion who brought race car coloring books.

I was happy to get to nationals but I was still not where I wanted to be. Winning a national title and leaving the sport on top was what I longed for.

Two wrestlers concerned me at nationals. They were Quincy Osborne from Augsburg College and Ricky Laforge, now wrestling for Delaware Valley College. This was over two years after Laforge's "senior night" at Hofstra University. When the seeds came back after an uneventful Thursday, Laforge was on my side of the bracket. He was the two seed, with Osborne occupying the top spot. I got the sixth seed and Gaeta was given the fourth.

The New England representative that year in the seeding meeting was Springfield College, Gaeta's coach. He told Coach Jones that Gaeta's previous three All-American awards carried more weight than my New England title and that was why he was given the higher seed. His main concern was that we did not have to wrestle each other in the quarterfinals. That made sense to me and I liked my spot in the bracket. At nationals all of New England becomes one team.

My opening round opponent was a bit of a surprise - Zach McKray from Wartburg College upset Zach Chambers from the University of Wisconsin at Platteville. Chambers had over thirty wins coming into nationals and McKray's record was 12-8. I was 46-3 and we were going to meet in the pre-quarterfinals. McKray was an All-American the previous year and had a much tougher schedule than the average Division III wrestler, and because of that, some people expected him to be victorious over me. The Iowa crowd seemed disappointed when I won, 5-0, to advance to the quarterfinals. There I expected to meet the number three seed, Paul LeBlanc from Cortland University in New York.

Once again, that match-up was not meant to be. This time it was LeBlanc who was upset by Minga Batsukh from St. John's College in Minnesota. Minga was only a freshman but was ranked third in the nation at one point during the year. He is a Mongolian citizen, and ironically was living with friends of mine in my hometown of Nutley, NJ prior to the season. In spite of who he was, first and foremost he was my opponent in the NCAA quarterfinals. I had to beat him.

When the match began, Minga pounded on my head relentlessly. I handled the pressure poorly. Instead of making my opponent react to me, I was reacting to Minga. Despite wrestling the match he wanted to, I took him down three times to win by a final of 8-6. The win assured me of All-American status.

Later on that day, while looking at the brackets posted in the hallway of the arena, Mike Gaeta's father strolled over. I told him, "Mike and I are going to have another match, this time for a national title." He was staring at our names and responded, "Wow, there you two are." I could detect a sense of pride, which I imagine only a parent can have. Then he said, "I certainly hope so." Back when I had defeated his son in the conference finals, Mr. Gaeta had congratulated me and gained my respect.

It was such a great feeling working out that night knowing only one match stood between me and the national finals. The 141 pound NCAA semifinals were Gaeta vs. the top seeded and number one ranked, Quincy Osborne, and me vs. the second seeded and ranked, Ricky Laforge.

While relaxing in my hotel room after the workout, I answered a phone call from my teammate, Martini. He had wrestled with Laforge for a year at Hofstra. It was not a call about strategy or advice. I wanted Martini's encouragement. In hindsight, it was a warning that my confidence level was not where it needed to be.

As soon as the semis began the next morning it was clear, the Gaeta vs. Bonora national finals was not going to happen. Within ten seconds, Gaeta was on his back fighting for his wrestling life. The final tally ended up, 15-3, in favor of Osborne. The score was really not an indication of how good a wrestler Gaeta was. I think his nerves got the best of him on that grand stage. Nerves can cause a loss just as easily as poor training.

The national semis were the biggest stage I had ever wrestled on. It was simultaneously an exciting and nerve racking experience. I wanted to get off to a quick start. Most wrestlers squander time during matches, especially at the beginning and end of periods. The beginning of the first is almost always wasted "feeling each other out." In addition, many wrestlers tend to slightly relax on the edge of the mat and it is easier to score. In the national semis against Laforge, I tried to take advantage of both of those bits of knowledge.

A minute into the match and not right away as I had planned, I shot my favorite shot, the low single. Once I captured his ankle, I made a huge mistake. Instead of bringing the leg instantly into the air, I stayed down on the mat. The blunder allowed Laforge to counter effectively and score two points. It would have been a crucial takedown and one that I felt I needed due to my lack of confidence. The majority of matches are won by the wrestler who scores the first takedown.

I reversed Laforge to tie the match at two. He escaped due to my subpar riding ability giving him a one point lead as the first period concluded. I chose bottom in the second and escaped again to tie the match. I did not attempt as many takedowns as I should have once we were on feet. Laforge shot a fireman's carry that I saw coming. I sprawled my legs back and tried to wrap him in a front headlock. He was stronger than me and was able to suck my leg up and finish another takedown.

Then so quickly, it was over. I ended up losing to the national runner up, 7-4. Laforge had pinned his first two opponents in less than one minute and thirty seconds combined. In the back of my mind, I did not really think I was better than him. Laforge was a name that I had heard my whole wrestling career, and his reputation and prominence really got the best of me. In retrospect, I could have won that match. All I had to do was wrestle with no fear. I should have done just that, since there was nothing for me to lose. The pressure was actually on him, he was supposed to beat me. After the loss I did not have much time to rebound as I was wrestling again within the hour.

As it happened, the wrestler Gaeta pinned in the quarterfinals, Jared Creason, was going to be my opponent. He had won a match the night before, after his loss. Then another one, while I was scrapping with Laforge. Not to take anything away from Creason, but it is hard to bounce back like I had to. He had already come to grips that the best he could do was take third, while I had only one hour to accept my situation. I was not mentally into the match from the start. I wrestled uninspired, while Creason, a senior from Coe College, was my polar opposite. The final score was 10-5, in his favor.

I really regret the way I performed in that match. Who knows, perhaps I would have won if I had wrestled with my heart in it. However, I cannot say that with any certainty. What I can say is that I would not have been as disappointed with the outcome.

Gaeta lost his wrestleback semifinals as well, which set up our third match in two weeks. Not for a national title, but for fifth place. It was not the way either of us had envisioned it the night before. Now, one of us was going to lose three consecutive matches in one day.

With the match only moments away, I overcame my disappointment and set out to win. The fifth place bout turned out exactly as its predecessors; two takedowns for the winner, and a final score of 6-5. This time it was Gaeta who came out on top. I thought I had a takedown at the end of the second period, but the referee did not give it to me. We had two controversial calls overall, and one went each way. All in all, I was proud because I knew I wrestled well. After the match we embraced one another and I congratulated Gaeta on an amazing career.

What You Can Take Away from Chapter 8:

1. Find ways to calm yourself down.

2. Make your opponent react to you, not the other way around.

3. A wrestling match is very short, do not waste any time.

4. Only do things that move you closer to your goal.

9

NUMBER ONE

The final chapter of my collegiate wrestling career started in Iowa the second after I lost to Gaeta. Due to my All-American status, I was able to walk on top of the NCAA podium for a split second. I eventually stopped at the spot I earned. It had the number six in front. But in my brief moment on top, I closed my eyes and envisioned myself there next year.

The Saturday night after the finals conclude, wrestlers, coaches, and family members tend to go out and celebrate. This usually is a night a wrestler looks forward to all season. On the contrary, the only thing on my agenda that night was a nice meal with my family. Afterward, I went back to my room and slept.

I would be graduating from RIC two months later, in May 2007, but since I had taken a year and a half off from wrestling, I still had twelve months of athletic eligibility. My options were few. The first was to wrestle at a Division I school. If I had won nationals my junior year, I would have went that route. Since I did not, my lone goal remained winning a Division III national title. An NCAA rule allows you only to continue wrestling for the Division III school at which you earned your undergraduate degree. This limited my Division III options to RIC.

Of course I had to be an enrolled student, and the next obstacle became getting into a graduate program at RIC. I had taken an undergraduate class in school psychology and liked it. After a lengthy application process I was accepted in the school psychology program and even managed to land a graduate assistantship position to pay for the tuition.

In the meantime, I was working out constantly. I knew I was going to find a way to compete and prepared accordingly. The New York Athletic Club (NYAC) became my training headquarters that entire summer. I remembered going to NYAC when I was a high school student and watching the national and world champs work out there. Now I was getting an opportunity to train alongside them and it felt great. On the other hand, before I actually got to the gym each time, I hated the idea of going. Then, following the workout, I was always glad I had gone, and felt something similar to a runner's high. The high was a mixture of being in New York City, working out diligently in the company of other serious athletes, and knowing I was doing everything I could to accomplish my goal.

In August of 2007, just before I was to head back to RIC to begin graduate school and resume my collegiate wrestling career, my girlfriend and I broke up after four years together. The next day at NYAC, I got beat up handily by lesser opponents. I wondered how my new relationship status would affect my wrestling, and that thinking in itself points to my one track mind. It was ironic since I had heard multiple times that girls are the fall of many great athletes. And yet, the exact opposite was happening to me. I was having trouble adjusting to my new life and as a result my wrestling suffered. It turned out to be a tough few weeks for me but I managed to get through it. Once I did, my wrestling was back on track as my then ex-girlfriend and I continued to talk on and off throughout the year.

As in previous summers, there were many things I wanted to work on before the season arrived and then set goals to continue improving as the season progressed. Here is a list I first made in the preseason of my junior year and continually modified, anytime I saw a crack in my wrestling.

Things I must work on during practice:

-Top: Riding Legs, Returning Opponents to the mat. Get nasty.
-Defense on my feet, get taken down too easily sometimes, Stay Focused.
-Defense to Legs
-Add ten pounds of muscle.
-Learn to deal with kids who attack your head better.
-DRILL TO THE FINISH EVERYTIME, Must finish shots cleanly, cannot hesitate.
-Practice Gator Roll, just in case.
-Finish opposite leg single from high crotch especially. If stuck circle left then cut back right while elevating opponent's leg.
-Don't finish dart shot coming out the back, finish it in front and bring it up. Or John Smith's finish.
-Drag like Casey
-Take shots with eyes closed and notice how it feels in the body.
-Never give up on Scrambles.
-Do chest passes with medicine ball, box jumps, sprint jump rope and sprints w/heavy bag
-LEAVE NO STONE UNTURNED
-Martini's single leg defenses A. whizzer own thigh, lock opponent's arm out if he reaches for the second leg, go with it and roll to his back. B. shoulder/head under chin
-Control Weight
-Outside Single
-Get Better every day.

Once school started I got on the mat as frequently as possible. I was curious to see what the freshmen had and who would be able to make an immediate impact. We were invited to help at a wrestling club in Johnston, Rhode Island, which was a great opportunity for our team. Wrestling with our future 133 and 149 pound wrestlers, Travis Drappi and Kevin Sutherland, led me to the conclusion that they both would be around .500 in their freshmen campaigns.

What I see now, that I did not then, was that the core group of freshmen showed up to every one of the preseason practices. They were willing to work hard to become better wrestlers. They were ready to pay their dues in the offseason, which is of utmost importance, and in myself I took that attitude for granted. It was nice to see these freshmen sharing those qualities. Sutherland eventually became the most vital person in the wrestling room to me, by becoming my new workout partner.

Before our first competition, the RIC team members were asked to officiate a takedown tournament for Rhode Island high school wrestlers. As one of the bouts was set to begin, the two wrestlers did the mandatory shaking of the hands, when one asked the other, "Are you good?" To which wrestler number two responded, "Um, yeah I think." Between the laughter, I blew the whistle to commence the highly anticipated match.

In preseason training I stumbled upon a problem that threatened my entire season. My right knee locked for the third time that preseason during a workout. Each time this happened, my knee was stuck in a bent position and I could not move it without pain. I had to build up my courage to extend my leg quickly and snap it back into place. An MRI of the knee revealed that I had lots of scar tissue that was throwing it out of whack. The doctor told me there was nothing he could do about it besides surgery. I decided not to let it bother me and went about my business, hoping it would not happen in any of my future matches.

One of the main areas of lifting I focused on during the offseason was my grip strength. Due to my Madelung's deformity, my wrists were still very weak. My friend, ex-coach and teammate, Keith had some serious grip strength which I envied. He could not curl twenty pounds or bench press half as much as me, but when we wrestled, he *felt* ten times stronger. I rock climbed in the summer to help build grip, finger and hand strength. I was also introduced by my friend, to a rotating grip-strength ball, which encourages gripping power and finger strength. I used it religiously.

The major influence on my grip strength was Andrew Algarin, who had been our heavyweight my junior year. He introduced me to the world's best grippers. At first, I could not even close the trainer, which required eighty pounds of pressure. My grip strength needed serious help and that is why I used a full gym day on it. It was a great decision and made me feel a lot stronger.

One day in September, I was told the number one nationally ranked 141 pound wrestler was: me. The rankings came from a great website that was new for the 2007-2008 season, d3wrestle.com. The rankings were not official, yet were almost identical to the NWCA rankings that would come out later in October.

When I my saw my name at the top of the list, I was a bit surprised. I had heard rumors that the defending 141 pound national champion was moving up a weight class, and I knew then that they were more than rumors. Robbie told me, "You better start working out harder now that you have a big bull's eye on your back." At first, the whole idea of being ranked first made me nervous. I told myself many times that it is just a ranking. Ultimately, I welcomed the big X. The thought, "Let them come," rang through my head. I took it one match, one period, one minute, one moment at a time, as former high school coach, Chris Chern told me to do.

The number one ranking was exciting yet at the same time, it put me on a bit of a pedestal in certain circles. It was hard to connect with my younger teammates, who only knew me by the ranking. They seemed to forget I was still going through the same struggles as them.

Wrestlers need their teammates. When there was distance between me and a teammate, I felt the gap needed to be closed. I knew I was going to have some close calls and that I would need their support and vice versa. Thankfully, I was surrounded by people who proved time and again that they would and could help me.

The weekend before our team's official practice was scheduled to start, I went home. My grandmother had been very sick and passed away while I was there. This was difficult for me to deal with even though she had been sick for a long time. I took comfort in the fact that her suffering was finally over. This also meant I would be staying home for the funeral services and would not be back at RIC to attend practice most of the crucial first week.

I did not get back to Rhode Island until late Thursday. In addition to feeling terrible about the loss of my grandmother, I felt bad that as a captain, I had not been there for the very beginning of the season. I also felt guilty that losing my grandma had already become just another situation which was negatively affecting my wrestling. Again it showed how the sport had consumed my life. I saw everything that happened in life in terms of whether or not it would affect wrestling. Sure, this showed dedication, but it also showed that I could have been giving wrestling too much power in my overall life.

I arrived at practice on the first Friday of the season, ready to go. Ideally, I would have a little over three weeks of mat time until the opening tournament. Realistically, I had much less time, due to my course schedule which caused me to miss quite a few practices.

This was part of being a wrestler *and* a graduate student. The classes I needed to take were only offered in the late afternoon from four to seven, or in the evening from seven to ten. Coach Jones was also an assistant football coach at nearby Bryant University, which practiced from four to six. This meant that during the first half of our season, wrestling practice was from six to eight thirty. On Mondays and Thursdays, I had a four to seven class, so I missed half the mat time. On Tuesdays, I had classes stretching from four in the afternoon to ten in the evening and consequently missed all of wrestling practice. One advantage was that I had no classes at all on Fridays.

Almost mockingly, while in one of my classrooms, I could see my team running outside through campus. Missing the run part of practice was not a big problem as it was the easiest thing to make up on my own. Still, I hated watching them through the window. I had to constantly remind myself that there was no other way. In time, the guys realized what room I was in and one day, as a joke, one of them screamed into the window, "Man I hate that I have herpes." All heads darted toward the window, a stunned look on everyone's face. I, on the other hand, could barely conceal my smile.

Missing a lot of practice was a major concern to me. To help make up for it, I worked out on my own, two to three times a day. However, nothing can get you into top wrestling shape except wrestling others. I was hoping my lack of mat time would not hurt me in the early part of the season. Twice a week I stayed late and wrestled more with former teammates Ray and Todd. They were both in the process of finishing up their degrees.

There were a few other things which were different about my senior year practices. First, we had only two official coaches in Jones and Paquette. Ray was the volunteer assistant. We also had changed the format of our Saturday morning practices. In previous years, early season Saturday practices were a split between the pool and the mat, but that year the three captains, along with the coaches, decided to make Saturdays a mock tournament day. It was designed to show the team the importance of warming up before matches.

Our team, like many, *mistakenly thought* that warming up would cause them to be too tired when a match began. I had learned that this was false. A college wrestling match is only seven minutes long. Our bodies can handle warming up while still competing at their highest level for that amount of time. The following experiment, which my team did on these Saturdays, proves it. We would wrestle a live bout as soon as practice began, then one in the middle and lastly, a third at the very end. Almost always the second match would turn out to be everyone's best. The first bout, when we were cold, was our worst. I am not suggesting an hour warm-up before a match. I am saying a wrestler *could* do that and still be fresh. We learned getting the first sweat out of our system before hitting the mat was best.

The weekend before the Roger Williams Invitational, we had our official mock dual meet. After seeing our team compete amongst ourselves, I thought we were going to be a middle of the pack team. I am glad to have been dead wrong.

I was very nervous because of my lack of practice time. I had also expected to win this tournament my junior year and had not even made the semis. In addition, I was wrestling with the target of number one ranking on my back for the first time. One comforting thought was that the tournament would be held in the same gymnasium where I had won a New England championship the previous February.

My first match was against a Bridgewater State freshman. Ray calmed me down when he said, "Go out there and show everyone why you are the best." He helped me recognize it was my opponent who should be nervous. On the flip side, my challenger may have thought to himself, "I have no pressure, he's supposed to beat me." Which is what I should have thought many times before.

Once I won the opening bout, my demeanor was more relaxed for the rest of the tournament and I won the invitational. When I evaluated my performance, I noticed a kink in my armor. I used the fireman's carry to score the majority of my takedowns. This was something my competition would also quickly notice, and I knew if I did not correct it, it could be troublesome in future matches. Overall, it was the start I expected for myself. My team, however, was a different story altogether.

I first noticed that we had a legitimate chance to win the tournament early in the day when Travis Drappi upset a returning All-New England wrestler. Going into the match, I did not think Travis had much of a chance. Keeping the ball rolling, another freshman, Kevin Sutherland upset Frank Cammisa, a defending New England champion. Sutherland went on to win in the finals by a major decision. Kevin Davis, our 197, coasted to his weight class crown as well.

Regardless of the individual performances, the story of the day was not any one of its parts, but RIC wrestling as a whole. We shocked everyone, including ourselves. We ended up in a tie for first place with the eighteenth ranked team in the country, despite not being ranked in the top thirty ourselves. It was the first time in fifteen years that RIC had won a tournament.

A few days later, Geoff Riccio, an injured member of our team, made the first of many extraordinary highlight videos. Getting to watch our achievements on film was as unexpected as the win. The highlights fired the guys up and became important to the future success of our team.

The new national rankings were announced the following Tuesday, with me at one, Sutherland at eight, and our team now ranked twenty-eighth in the country. Oddly, we did not believe our collective success would last, even though we did believe in ourselves as strong competitors individually. We did not talk about it much, having confidence in ourselves was enough.

In between the first two tournaments we had a dual match in Boston against MIT. Normally their team is not the most competitive due to the rigors of their students' academic workload. (Ironically at the 2008 NCAA championships, they finished fifteenth in the nation on the strength of their heavyweight wrestler, Glen Geesemen, despite an 0-22 record as a team). The dual match should have been painless for us. It did not turn out that way. We were overconfident as a whole after our impressive performance a few days earlier at Roger Williams. Our team wrestled terribly and we were lucky to escape with a win.

The next tournament, the Doug Parker Invitational at Springfield College, was a bigger test for us than Roger Williams Invitational. When I calculated our chances of winning, I came up with zero percent. I tried to focus on myself because I knew there would be tougher competition than I had faced in the brief season. My bracket had thirty-one wrestlers in it, as teams were allowed to enter more than one athlete per weight. The problem for us was that we only had fourteen wrestlers total.

Out of fourteen, eight placed to help us win the tournament, which was another pleasant shock.

It was at this tournament where I decided I had to get more physical during my matches. The objective was to beat my opponents so badly that they never wanted to wrestle me again. Not to hurt them, just to take them out of their comfort zone.

In the semifinals, I wrestled a freshman who was a New Jersey state finalist the year before. Going into the match I had more butterflies than normal. I had only taken eighth in the state. My game plan was to be very physical with him. In the beginning of the match, he shot in and I secured a front headlock. I locked it up tight and then bounced his head off the mat. He was stunned and I easily spun around for the takedown. The exchange set the tempo for the whole match. The final score was 18-6 in my favor. I won the next match as well and became the tournament champion.

It is important to know that every wrestler has a breaking point. Everyone eventually will mentally and physically give up. I breached that with my opponent in the semifinals soon after the first takedown. At that point, he stopped trying to win the match and only concerned himself with making it until the end.

When you have two champions going at it, you usually do not see it occur, though it certainly is possible. This happened to me when I was broken by Gaeta during my freshman year. When beaten that way, all a wrestler wants to do is crawl into a corner and cover his head, feeling helpless, hopeless, and embarrassed. No one ever *wants* it to happen. On the other hand, an athlete gains a lot through the learning and growth which occurs by experiencing that breaking point, and in the end it may actually be beneficial. What I gained by my experience was mental toughness. During my senior year, I told myself if I was ever down by ten points, I would still come after my opponent to try for a fall. I would never give up.

Our team had one more tournament to wrestle before the first semester concluded. Each of the three tournaments was progressively more challenging than the previous one and the Rochester Invitational was easily the toughest of the three. The field was made up of mostly teams from New Jersey, New York,

Pennsylvania, and Ohio, including three teams ranked in the top twenty. To lessen our chances even more, we were not going to be able to enter a 174 pound wrestler, with both Brendan Casey and Joe Manley sidelined. They had placed third and fifth respectively at Springfield.

We were now only able to enter twelve wrestlers. Our diminished numbers, compounded with the level of competition, led us to believe that our short, wild ride as tournament victors was about to come to an end. Then, Brendan Guarino and Ray Moore stepped up and placed for the first time that year. We had three champions (Martini, Logan, and myself) in the ten weight classes, and out of our twelve guys, eight medaled. What that meant was we had won back to back to *back* tournaments. Afterward, RIC moved up to rank eighteen in the nation. We finished the first half of the season 3-0 in dual meets, while winning all the tournaments we entered.

I had made it through unscathed. For the next semester, as a graduate assistant, I took only two classes and was able to choose classes on Monday and Tuesday nights. Since football season was over, practice time moved to four to six thirty and I would not miss anymore practices the rest of the season. I was psyched.

I was still on good terms with my then ex-girlfriend and confided in her that my main concern heading into the second semester was my weight. "You better not let that be an excuse," she said, and recommended that I start writing down everything I ate. The idea was that when I saw in print the amount of food I was consuming, it would help curb my appetite. Although at first it sounded crazy, her idea worked. I also added to the journal my weight each morning and every workout I did. My "food folder" was very useful on days before matches. I was able to see exactly what I ate, how much I worked out and what the results were. Looking back on it now, the whole thing seems a bit much. Nonetheless, it was what I needed to do, to address my problem of overeating.

What You Can Take Away from Chapter 9:

1. Accept unchangeable circumstances and adjust to make up for them.

2. If you want something bad enough, you have to make it your number one priority.

3. Whatever scenario you find yourself in, you can draw a mental edge from it.

4. Write down what you have to improve.

10

MIDLANDS

RIC wrestling was on a break from December 7, 2007 to January 11, 2008. Coach Jones had planned three different trips to tournaments throughout the country in order to fill in for the lack of matches. Unfortunately, none of them panned out because of financial reasons. That left the RIC team idle for five weeks.

That could have been disastrous. Fortunately for me, the opportunity arose to compete at Midlands "45" in late December. The tournament was the best in the nation on the Division I level. Because our team was under the allowed competition dates, I did not have to sit out any RIC matches in order to attend Midlands. Once I knew I could go without hurting my team, it came down to making the right decision for me.

I understood that other Division III wrestlers competed against better competition throughout the year than I was able to. That gave them a distinct advantage over me. If I went to Midlands, the gap between matches would be bridged and I would also get a chance to experience the difference between divisions. In the past there had been Division III champions who went on to win the Division I nationals.

On the other hand, I wanted to have a perfect season and if I went to Midlands and lost, that goal would be gone. There was something mystical about ending a year undefeated. Accepting the invitation might turn into a major hurdle I would be voluntarily forcing myself to overcome.

In the end, I decided to take that chance. It is better to lose a match or two during the season, than to go into nationals undefeated and leave differently. As Tom Ryan told me while I was at Hofstra, "We learn a lot more from our losses than our wins." I was still looking to learn.

My father and brother, Robbie, made the journey with me to Chicago. I was on my own with no coach in my corner, just my brother encouraging me and my dad videotaping. Robbie did an awesome job and when I watch the tapes and listen back to the matches, I realize he had a lot of useful suggestions. I guess all of those years of watching his older brothers wrestle had taught him well.

I had no one to drill with and that was a major problem. Drilling is such important preparation for successful wrestling in competition. Luckily Ben Hoover, a fellow Division III wrestler, recognized me from nationals the previous season. "I remember your hunchback," he said. That gave me a good laugh. My back had caused me a lot of pain over the years and I was glad some good came out of it.

The day before the tournament, I was six pounds over. The Christmas feast, had only been three days before. Also one of the downsides of the sport, the skin ailment ringworm, had sidelined me two weeks prior to the holiday. I was therefore not able to practice much leading up to Midlands. Two weeks off before the toughest wrestling tournament in my life was not a situation I relished being in, but it was where I found myself.

I lost three pounds at the workout with Ben and then drank a bottle of water, which put me back to four pounds over. By my second workout, I weighed 144.5. I lost the remaining weight in the hotel workout room. After a bottle of ice water I went to bed knowing that my body would "float" the added water weight by morning. I knew it was too much weight to cut the day before a tournament but the skin infection had handcuffed me.

I woke up exactly 141.0. I weighed in and started to get into my routine. My first match was against the number seven seed, CJ Ettelson. I was unseeded. An older gentleman from the Iowa area sought me out to say that it was going to be a good match. That one line gave me confidence and reminded me that I belonged there.

I took Ettelson down with three different fireman's carries. Powered by those takedowns, I beat him, 9-4. My bracket was huge and to win it, I was going to have to duplicate my success five more times.

My second round opponent was Keith Sulzer from Northwestern. The same inexcusable mistake I made in 2006 against Mike Conklin was about to bite me again. I overlooked him. He was unseeded and I had just beaten a ranked wrestler. On the Division I level, seeds do not matter as much. (As Ettelson would prove later in the year when he defeated the number one ranked Division I wrestler, 9-3.) Sulzer had a bye in the first round and therefore had the luxury of watching my battle with Ettelson. He knew all about my fireman's carry. The opportunity to strike with it never arose in my match with Sulzer.

Following a 2-2 first period, Sulzer rode me out the whole second period, giving him a point advantage. My riding ability was subpar at best. I chose to let him up at the beginning of the third. Now, I was losing 4-2. The idea was to wait until there was about thirty seconds left before I tried to score a takedown. Then in all probability I would ride him out for the rest of the period and force overtime. At the premeditated time I struck, got in very deep and had him on his butt. He was lanky and tied me up until time expired. After eighteen straight wins, I had lost the first match of my senior season.

The entire third period, Robbie was screaming from my corner, "Shoot!" Even though I heard him, my thought was that, "he doesn't know what he's talking about." In this situation,

Robbie proved to be correct. I realized that my third period approach was not well thought out. You cannot afford to waste any time during a wrestling match. And the thing that took way too long for me to learn was that I could never overlook anyone. I already knew this on an intellectual level, but the problem was that simply telling yourself something is much different than actually following through with it.

I did not know it at the time, but the loss to Sulzer would turn out later to be the *best* thing that could have happened to me.

Despite the important lessons, I fell into my usual funk after a loss. It was the price I paid for wanting to win every tournament. My third match was against a wrestler from Rider University. Before the bout I thought, "If I just lose now I could not worry about wrestling or making weight the rest of the weekend." I was looking for an out. My excuse would have been "I would've beaten that guy if we had wrestled in the winner's bracket." I did not think this on a conscious level, yet I know it was there.

The match began with a hand slap from Robbie. Even with my negative thinking I scored two quick takedowns and was winning, 4-1. Then I took my foot off the gas. For whatever reason, I was content with leading when I should have had a killer instinct and broken my opponent when I had the chance. Instead, I wrestled too cautiously after I had built a lead and was unable to step up when the pressure was on. He closed the gap though I held on for a 5-3, win.

The way to wrestle is always with relentless pressure. For most of the season I did exactly that, but at Midlands, I faltered because I was not confident enough. The victory over my Rider counterpart set up a match with Drew Headlee from Pittsburgh.

During the Headlee match, there were two key scrambles. They both went his way and I ended up on my back for two seconds following one of them. The final tally was 10-4, in his favor. If I had gotten the takedown instead of going to my back it would have been tied at six. Moments make matches.

My Midlands experience was over. I had wrestled against some of the best wrestlers in the country at the Division I level. Dedication, hard work, and sacrifice are qualities that lead to success on any level of athletics. Looking back on the tournament, I could have won if I had gone in with the right attitude and wrestled well. That fact gives me a tremendous sense of pride and shows the importance of one's mentality.

While my family and I were out to dinner that night, I explained my frustration with the way the tournament went. My dad responded, "Mike, you did not come here to win, you came here to lose, now don't let it happen again." My father had seen right through me. My purpose for going *had* been to learn, and not really to win. In one sense, I was successful because I did learn quite a bit, but I recognized that what my father said was right as well -- always go to win. Yet for me, the bottom line for Midlands "45" was that I made the right move by going to Chicago.

The final bout of Midlands was the last live match Robbie ever saw me wrestle. He departed soon after for a semester abroad, and left me a letter. It was sealed, and on the front in big bold letters was written, "Do Not Open Until Iowa." Iowa was where the 2008 NCAA Division III Wrestling Championships were going to be held. I was extremely tempted to tear the letter open. Thankfully, I combated my impulses. The letter's home for the next few months was on the wall above my calendar with a thumbtack stabbed through its heart. Robbie was one of four people who wrote me inspirational notes throughout college. The other three were Ray, my girlfriend Christina, and my former coach, Chris Chern. They combined to pen many letters to me throughout my career, which touched me deeply. All were somehow different in what they wrote, yet every letter always seemed to say exactly what I needed to hear at the time. I read them before every remaining match of my career and many times between. The letters were inspirational, confidence building, reassuring, and most importantly positive.

In this sport you cannot do everything on your own.

As soon as I flew back to New Jersey, I put the Midlands tournament behind me, although I was very upset that my "perfect" season did not come to fruition. Honestly, I had come to grips with the idea that it might happen, even before I had left for Chicago. It was time to reassess myself completely and "leave no stone unturned." I had only one semester of wrestling left in my life and I was determined not to deal with another loss.

Before it was time to head back to Rhode Island, I continued double session workouts in New Jersey. And as did most of the civilized world, I went out on New Year's Eve. No alcohol was ingested although I was now over twenty-one. The year before, I had taken a shot of tequila and while it probably did not hurt my wrestling, physically or mentally, it definitely did not help.

An athlete should only try to do things that improve their chances of winning. Alcohol definitely does not fit into that philosophy. To some extent, wrestling is not like baseball or football. Those guys may be able to party during their season and compete at close to their highest level. Wrestlers cannot do that, no matter what they think. The ones who do, make it clear that partying is more important to them than accomplishing their goals. They may not admit it, but that is the bottom line.

On a practical level, drinking is detrimental to a wrestler's weight. Drinking during the season only serves as a possible excuse for losing; an out. There is such a small window to accomplish great feats in athletics, especially wrestling. Drinking and partying close that window much quicker than nature eventually will. The season is less than five months each year and four years of college eligibility is all anyone gets. In my mind, to waste any of that time would have been a sin.

What You Can Take Away from Chapter 10:

1. You make excuses to yourself just as often as to others.

2. A rule of thumb in training -- take the path of most resistance.

3. Do not wait to score, do it when you can.

4. Be grateful to the people who make sacrifices for you.

11

ADVERSITY

The team headed back to school on January 3, 2008. We had double session practices until classes began nineteen days later. It was during this break in scholastic semesters when our team building typically occurred. The only students on campus were athletes and as a team we saw each other at least five hours a day. Our numbers were already very low and we could not afford to lose anyone else. Luckily for our team we had Nick Logan. Everyone on the team connected with Logan, whether young or old, inexperienced or a seasoned veteran, he was the glue that held us together, the bridge between old and new. All teams need someone like him.

The second semester saw the addition of another coach, Bob Smith, arguably the greatest wrestling coach in Rhode Island history. At Coventry High School he won seventeen consecutive state titles and earned the Coach of the Decade award for the 1990s. One time early in his return to our team, he was the only instructor at practice and gave the most inspirational speech I have ever heard. The team's favorite quote from it was, "You've got to look the devil in the eye, shoot a blast double on him and tell'im to go to hell." He was such an asset for the younger wrestlers and a perfect fit for a team that was already doing so well.

In spite of the good atmosphere in our wrestling room, our additional coach, and our sensational first semester, my faith in the team was low. We were young, inexperienced, and lacked depth, a combination which usually spells disaster. Many things had to go right to accomplish our team goal of winning a New England title. One injury to any starter and our dream would pop faster than a bubble. The starting ten, in order, was: Hoyt, Drappi, Bonora, Sutherland, Martini, Guarino, Casey, Logan, Davis, and Moore. Four of the ten were freshmen. We had three backups in Ryan Hardy, Joe Manley, and Chris Dean at 125, 174, and 197 respectively.

After working hard during the double sessions, we were starving for a chance to begin wrestling other teams again. The national duals at Lycoming College were going to be a huge test for us. There were multiple teams ranked in the top ten and more than ten in the top thirty, including RIC. In my weight class the fourth, sixth, and eighth ranked wrestlers would be looking to knock me off. The way the chips fell, I ended up wrestling number eight, Luke Baum.

In our two previous matches he had never taken me down. I was confident.

When our bout began, Baum scored a takedown right away and took control of the match. I was on bottom, losing 3-1 with a minute left in the final period. I looked up into the stands and saw the New York team, Cortland, cheering for my opponent. I understood that people enjoy an upset. Even so, I had worked very hard to achieve my ranked position and this one loss could tear everything down. I thought, "What am I doing? I have to win this match." I escaped and got a takedown right on the line to win by one point.

I learned from that match just how big that X on my back was. Of course I had known all season it was there, but I had not realized the extent of what it meant. Baum had a lot of videotape on me from our previous matches and had clearly studied it well. I also watched those tapes, but did not analyze it the way he did. That tends to happen in all sports. The favorite watches the film just as the underdog does, but each watches with a very different perspective and for a different reason.

Aside from my scare, our team wrestled an excellent tournament. We beat three teams which were ranked in the top fifteen in the country -- York College, Ithaca College, and The College of New Jersey (TCNJ). Before the season, if someone told me that RIC would beat TCNJ in a wrestling match, I would have laughed. With a few Jersey boys on their side, RIC did do it. One in particular, Brendan Guarino, pulled through with one of the biggest pins of the season. Then Davis glued his foe's shoulders to the mat to seal our win. Our reaction in a candid team photograph says it all. I jumped four feet off the ground.

We placed fifth in the tournament, as we suffered our first loss of the season to Loras College, 20-19. With our 4-1 mark, I finally knew that our team was not a New England fluke. If we stayed healthy, we were going to be the favorites to win the NEWA Championships in late February.

I recognized following the team tournament, that there was a lot of work for me to do before nationals. I also became aware that Lycoming was the last place on the regular season schedule, where I would wrestle anyone who was nationally ranked. From January 13 until March 6, the only wrestlers I would face were on New England teams.

The 141 pound weight class in New England was much different in 2008 than 2007. There were plenty of tough wrestlers, just none the caliber of those I had previously encountered -- Gaeta (four-time All-American), Lacroix (third place finisher in the NCAAs), Marsh (All-American) and Conklin (two-time national qualifier). I had to rely heavily on my teammates to help me improve. The one guy I leaned on the most was Martini. I also counted on my accumulated knowledge over the years to help pull me through as I read and reread the notes I had written to myself.

Our next match of note occurred at the New England duals where RIC was the number one seed. On that particular

Sunday, our two other team captains, Casey and Davis, were out of the lineup. Even with both of those great wrestlers, we did not match-up well against the number two seed, J-Wu. It was going to take a miracle to win the tournament.

We headed into the first match-up with J-Wu in the team tournament final coming off three wins. It was not pretty for the RIC Anchormen. Our whole team wrestled terribly, losing eight of the ten weights. Looking at the positive side, our second place finish was the highest in RIC's history at that particular tournament.

My next bout of significance would come against a Division II team. The previous year against this same team, I had beaten my opponent by nine points. That fact did not bring me much comfort because two of my three takedowns came via the fireman's carry. I knew my adversary would shut that down this time around.

As I expected, our second meeting was much more difficult. Now I ask myself, was it more difficult simply because I thought it was going to be? Oddly, it seemed to me that he was content just keeping the score close. I was winning by one with a minute left and he took a single shot during the final seconds of the match. He was stalling, so I won.

Occasionally, wrestlers encounter an opponent who clams up and tries to keep the score close. No great upsets ever happen with that strategy. Until the 2007-2008 season, my opponents always came after me. Wrestling aggressively against me, played into my advantage. I scored at least half of my takedowns off of my opponents' attempts. Once they began to employ avoid tactics, it was difficult to adjust. In the back of my mind I had to keep telling myself, "When you get to nationals, no one will run." It was important not to change drastically against these types of wrestlers. If I did, it would have opened holes in my defense that more skilled opponents could capitalize on. I knew my brand of wrestling, highly offensive with a solid defense, would be successful against the competition I would encounter in Iowa.

What added to the difficulty of the situation was the competency of the rival coaches. They had scouted me very well. Constantly the screams from opposing corners were, "Here comes the dart" referring to my low single or, "Watch the fireman's." It was very frustrating and limited the use of my two most effective moves. My objective during matches now was to avoid putting myself in danger. In my mind, even if the scores were close, if I was never out of position or in jeopardy of being taken down, I could not lose.

It was about this time when Martini introduced me to one of the toughest things I have ever done. We simply referred to it as "The Run." It consists of putting the treadmill up to the speed of ten miles per hour and running at least three miles. When he first urged me to do it, I was hesitant. Eventually, I succumbed to his pressure and ran at that speed for over twenty minutes. Every second was painful, but the sense of accomplishment when I was finished was worth the constant discomfort. Next time, it was four miles in twenty-four minutes. The plan was to push myself to five miles in thirty minutes.

The idea was cut short when I strained ligaments on the outer part of my right foot in early February. I did however catch a nice break. Once in my stance, the pain magically disappeared. It must have seemed very peculiar to others that I limped to the mat, yet did not skip a beat once on it.

Brendan Casey's father passed away right after my injury. As expected, the passing was tremendously hard for him. Athletes might have to deal with loss at some point in their career. Their performance depends on their state of mind. Some can use the competition as an emotional escape or release. Others use it as a distraction. A few continue to compete because they think their loved one would have wanted it that way. On the other side of the coin, some people see no point in playing a game when a loved one has just left this earth. When my brother's best friend, Sam Hernandez tragically died, Robbie had no desire to play a high school basketball game. It all depends on your personality and no way is the right way.

Personally, I was lucky not to have dealt with that kind of tragedy during my competition schedule. My grandmother passed away a month before the first tournament of my senior year. I had enough time to get into the right mindset before the opening meet. Casey handled his situation much better than I think I could have. After five days at home, he returned to school and I asked him how he was doing.

He responded, "It sucks, but I'm not going to sit around and feel sorry for myself. My father wouldn't want me to be sulking for him."

The response surprised me slightly and increased (if that was possible) my respect for Casey. Life throws you some nasty pitches and sometimes you have to swing even if the ball is in the dirt. This was one of those instances and Casey did not let it beat him.

Despite our lopsided loss, the RIC and J-Wu dual was a highly anticipated match between the thirteenth and fourteenth ranked teams in the country. Besides being cross town rivals, Lonnie Morris, the J-Wu head coach, and his assistant, Brian Allen, had been teammates with Coach Jones on the championship teams of RIC's past. I was confident we could turn it around and win, as my team did in 2004 against them to earn the league title.

The buildup finally came to head on February 12, 2008, when we drove to the other side of Providence. We were now the underdogs and favored only at two of the ten weights. We started the match with Drappi upsetting his opponent by decision. I was up next and won 15-3, but not by fall as I was hoping. At 149, Sutherland did more than expected and won by a major decision. After three matches, we were up 11-0. We needed a stick from Martini, as he had done the previous season against his rival.

This time, Martini was on his back within thirty seconds. Without much more scoring, the J-Wu wrestler held on for the win. The loss shifted the momentum. The final score was 22-11, in favor of J-Wu. Even if Martini had pinned, we would have still came up a bit short.

RIC had no reason to be ashamed. Everyone wrestled well and it was one of those rare situations where we lost and did not leave feeling like losers. They were a better dual meet team than us. Regardless, I was still convinced that in ten days, when the conference championships commenced, we would prevail. We were a tournament team and a team that I believed would place all ten guys at the championships. I felt that we were the only team with a shot at doing that.

The last dual meet for RIC's three captains took place on February 15, 2008. Knowing that I would never again wrestle in front of some great people, choked me up a bit before the last home match at the Murray Center.

Senior night was a great night of wrestling. First our team shut out Trinity College. Then we crushed the number four team in New England, Bridgewater State, whom we had edged only by a point at the New England duals.

For these two final matches, I decided to switch something that wrestlers do not tend to change -- my wrestling shoes. The ones I had previously worn had never found a place in my heart as all my previous pairs. My friend, Colin, still had the same style shoes I had worn out my freshman year of college, the gray and blue Sydney 2000s. In my opinion they were second only to the black and teal, Smith Elite Internationals. I constantly searched the web for either of those two shoes to no avail. One day I noticed that Colin wore my exact shoe size. I decided to ask if he would let me borrow the shoes for the stretch run. He readily handed them over and I gladly slipped on those shoes for every match from then on. While their grip may not have been what it once was, peace of mind that I was comfortable in my shoes trumped the traction.

Superstitions are commonplace among athletes. I used to be very superstitious in high school. By the time I was heading into my senior year of college, I tried to limit them as much as possible. I did not want to have any excuses for why I did not win a match. To break superstitions I purposely would do things differently. I convinced myself superstitious beliefs had nothing to do with the outcome of matches. I did not listen to the same music, perform the same warm-ups, or say the same prayers. That is why I was able to switch my shoes. The most important thing is one's performance on the mat. I knew by then that what socks I was wearing would not affect the outcome of a match and that if I let it, it might mentally ruin me.

Following senior night, there were only two tournaments left of my career. The pressure on me was slowly building all season, leading to this conclusion. I felt it from the time I learned I was the top ranked wrestler in the nation at my weight class. In the beginning, I kept telling myself to take it one match at a time. I tried not to look at what the ramifications might be if I lost. To counter the pressure I would think to myself, "If I wrestle to the best of my ability, I cannot be beaten." Even if that was not true, it was comforting to feel as if everything was in my own hands. As the season wore on, I started to like the pressure. I liked to overcome it and I almost miss it now. There was something about being in those situations that made me feel electric. It excited me when I was in a position where everyone's eyes were focused on my every move, like a gladiator in the Coliseum of antiquity.

All athletes should want to feel pressure. Great wrestlers want to be in a tied match with a few seconds left. They enjoy that moment, it is well-earned and athletes deserve to revel in that feeling. There is no gratification in doing something that comes easily. The pins and technical falls were not my proudest moments. What I prided myself on, was when the chips were down and I was losing in the third period, I had the heart to keep on fighting. When a wrestler can envision himself in that type of situation before it happens, he will be much better off when they do occur. Getting nervous and thinking panicked thoughts such as "Oh my God this is it, I have to do this," causes negative things to happen.

The practice week before the conference championships was always a special time. Everyone always seems to give it their all when they see the light at the end of the tunnel. For most, it was the end of a long journey started five months earlier. The majority of wrestlers on our team did not qualify for nationals.

Thinking back, it is a shame I could not stop and savor the moment more. My eyes were set on a national title and nothing was going to cloud them.

Most people thought I had nothing to worry about at the conference championships. That was untrue. My nerves were just as jumpy as anyone else's. In my head I pictured what would happen if I lost, despite preparing for success. It was easy to see how my story could have had a different ending. It could have been: Number one in the country going in, fourth in conference going out. As quickly as possible I tried to rid myself of the negative thoughts. Besides those feelings, prior to the NEWA Championships, I also had to deal with a physical problem.

The day of the final practice I was feeling a bit under the weather. I had to go to the campus health service center anyway to get a note for scars left from the ringworm I had battled before Christmas. I was taking no chances with not being allowed to wrestle. Standard procedure at the health center was to take a temperature on every patient. When the thermometer clicked in my ear, it read 101.6. The nurse practitioner told me, "You can't wrestle in the tournament, so there's no reason to get a note for the scars."

I laughed out loud. If a fever would be enough to stop me from entering the New England tournament, I probably would have never wrestled at the collegiate level to begin with. I realized it was no joke when she said, "Michael, I know this is important to you, but you have the flu and it will get worse over the weekend." As calmly as I could, I explained that if I did not wrestle in this tournament, I would never be able to live with myself. We finally agreed that I would take my own temperature before each match. If it was over 100, I would not compete. While nodding my head in agreement, I tried to control my smile. She loaded me up with thermometers I had no intention of using. Then, she instructed me to tell Coach Jones to call her and to take ibuprofen every four hours. Following our agreement, she wrote the note for the scars. As I walked out, I thought, "This just got a lot harder."

On the drive up to the University of Southern Maine where the championships were held, I mapped out my game plan. I knew I was not going to have optimal capacity in my lungs. The idea was to build an early lead before hitting cruise control. That plan was not going to contribute to winning a team title. I knew I had to tell my coaches about my situation. It did no one any good if the coaches were yelling to keep attacking, when I had to save myself for the next matches. Out of everyone, Ray seemed the most nervous although he managed to say, "We'll get through this." Every four hours I ingested ibuprofen, cough medicine, and inhaled plenty of nose drops, though I never did use those thermometers.

To make matters worse, I had to wrestle five matches instead of four, as I did the previous year. The top seed does not automatically get a bye in college tournaments. I reminded myself of what my high school coach, Mr. Lore, always used to say about wrestling matches. "You can do anything for six minutes" (make that seven minutes in college). While that was true, I knew I would have to win three matches on the first day and two on the second, *if* I won them all. I tried to stay positive and told myself I was lucky the flu struck the weekend of the conference championships instead of just before nationals.

I continued to repeat in my head, "All that matters is to win and advance." It was not important if I was impressive in doing so. I told the coaching staff my idea of starting strong and then protecting and they agreed it was the best bet. Now the plan of attack was different though the goal remained constant: Make it through the tournament intact, get to nationals and win a title there.

There were obvious dangers in my game plan for the 2008 NEWA Championships. If coaches or competitors on the other teams picked up what was going on, I would be vulnerable to a constant attack from my opponents, aiming to wear me down. I did not want anyone to figure out that I was sick. At first, this circle of trust did not even include my parents. My reasoning for keeping them in the dark was to keep *their* nerves in check.

My parents were suspicious from the get-go. I had to reassure them I was fine until they finally conceded the point. That was, until our 133, Travis Drappi, accidentally slipped and asked them how I was feeling. My parents responded with slight bewilderment, "What do you mean? He's not okay?" In typical Drappi fashion, he said, "Uh oh, was I not supposed to tell you?"

When the qualifier got underway our team's diminished numbers did not matter anymore. It was our best ten guys versus everyone else's best ten. Due to my health I was not going to be able to stick around and support my teammates as much as I would have liked. I felt terrible about that. My teammates understood the situation and knew when the season is on the line, each individual athlete has to come through for himself.

Within seconds of my first match, I was taken down by an opponent whom I had beaten by twelve points, only two weeks prior. The first thought to pop into my head was, "This is going to be really hard."

Ray later told me, "I thought that was it, I thought you were going to lose and were not going to have enough strength to wrestleback. Then I kept telling myself no, he worked too hard, he won't lose now."

My next thought during the bout, "He is not going to roll over." Not many wrestlers do in the conference championships. I regrouped and pinned him.

During my second match I felt awful with the nastiest "cotton mouth" of my life. If you do not know what "cotton mouth" is, you are lucky. It normally occurs when you are almost completely dehydrated and there is no saliva left in your mouth. When this happens even the simplest tasks become difficult. I managed to get through the quarterfinals with a sloppy performance, and moved to the semifinals. Joining me as semifinalists were seven of my teammates, meaning that eight RIC wrestlers placed in the tournament. It was not the ten we were hoping for, still it was a very respectable showing.

In my third and final match of the day, I won by three points. The next positive for RIC came at 157. The match had huge team ramifications, as it pitted a wrestler from the first and second place squads. Martini squared off against his J-Wu counterpart, who had beaten him in the dual two weeks earlier. Now in a much more significant bout than their previous meeting, Martini won by a pin in the first period.

At 197 we had a similar scenario, except Kevin Davis had never beaten Diego Crespo. Crespo was a defending New England champion and had been a New Jersey state champion in high school. We hoped Davis could find a way to succeed when we needed him so badly. During an upper-weight clinch thirty seconds into the match, Davis decked Crespo with a lateral drop that shocked the gym. The win could not have come at a better time, and the match became the highlight of the tournament for our team.

What was even more impressive about Davis's pin was that he was dealing with health issues too, and was not medically cleared to wrestle until our drive up to the University of Southern Maine. Two days prior to the journey, he had seriously injured his right knee and could barely walk. The doctors said that they would not allow him to wrestle due to a potential tear of his ligaments (it did end up being a meniscus tear, which later required surgery). He was finally cleared because at that time, he had not taken an MRI that would have revealed the tear.

With the conclusion of the first day of the tournament, J-Wu was one point ahead of us. J-Wu had eight wrestlers left vying for the top spot, just as we did. Three RIC guys were on the winner's side of the bracket with Martini, Davis, and me, all in the first finals. The rest of our team could still win their individual brackets with a lot more work.

My first finals the next morning was against Matt Ulrich from the host school, Southern Maine. I was still battling the effects of flu but knew I had to tough it out two more times to advance to nationals. The plan was to physically beat him up in the opening moments of the match in order to break his spirits and take away any opportunity for his fans to cheer. I started strong with a quick takedown and kept the pressure on him for as long as I could. The final score was 9-3 in my favor.

The winner of the first finals did not have to wrestle again for more than seven hours. I used that time to sleep. I did not bother to stick around and see who would come through to wrestle me in the "real finals." My guess was I would face Ulrich again, since he had beaten the third ranked Dylan Rittenburg twice. I had wrestled both of them already and did not need to scout anymore. Either way, I knew I had to win the next match, no matter who I was wrestling. That is the mindset every wrestler should have at all times.

Martini gutted out a victory in the first finals with his second overtime win in three matches. Davis's fate was unfortunately different. Maybe it was his knee, who knows, since he would never use that as an excuse. When he lost the first finals, he had to wait and see who the winner of the wrestleback bracket would be. To no one's surprise it was Crespo. On his way to the title, Crespo ended up edging Davis in what I was told was a great match.

Day two of the NEWA Championships turned out to be RIC's shining moment. The guys in the wrestleback brackets collected three third place finishes, two fourths, and a fifth. Their performances meant the fate of the team title rested on the matches Martini and I would each wrestle. When Coach Jones told us that, it pumped me up even more. My goal now became to earn a major decision and ensure an extra team point, just in case Martini faltered.

My assumption that Ulrich would win was incorrect as Rittenburg came back to beat him. It set up a rematch of the Springfield tournament finals that occurred three months prior. In that match, I had won, 10-5. Rittenburg already had proven that regular season matches could not foretell future knockout bouts contested under much more pressure. I knew that the outcome of our previous match meant nothing. All that mattered was this one.

Walking in I noticed a spotlight hanging from the center of the gym. The fans were boisterous and ready for the finals to start. I walked slowly as my name was called to meet in the middle of the mat for the pre-match introductions.

As the 2008, 141 pound New England title bout began, my adrenaline was pumping so much that I did not feel any effects of my flu. With thirty seconds left in the finals, I had built a five point lead, which was not enough for a major decision. What I needed was a takedown straight to my opponent's back. Then, it happened. Rittenburg went for a five point throw to tie. That was his only option. I was ready for it. I caught him on his back for two seconds. The referee awarded me the takedown and two back points as time expired. I celebrated more after that match than any other in my entire career.

Martini's match was another nail biter. Neither finalist could gain the upper hand by the end of regulation. They had a scoreless neutral overtime, then the situation worked in Martini's favor as it was his third match to reach that junction in the tournament. As in his previous matches, he escaped and then rode out his foe to win in the tiebreaker period, somehow winning the tournament, by collecting only one takedown in all four of his matches *combined*. He knew his strengths and used them well. I had never seen him that happy.

Only weeks before, Martini had been ranked in the country for the first time. That pumped him up and helped him win a New England title. A wrestler has to use everything available to his advantage, whether it is being angry over not being ranked or using the rankings to get into a better mindset. When Martini won the 157 pound title, we knew that RIC had clinched the team championship.

Before the announcement of team champions, I felt like a little kid on his way into Disney World for the first time. When the announcement finally boomed over the public address system that RIC was the NEWA Champion, the feeling of euphoria continued and grew. Having only fourteen guys on a team and winning the title in the way we did had been unthinkable at the beginning of the season. Jones and Paquette were given the head and assistant Coach of the Year awards, respectively. I would later tell Casey and Davis, "We 'old' guys, led a bunch of kids to the 'Promised Land,' and I hope they enjoyed it half as much as we did."

The good feelings did not last long for me as the flu kicked into high gear, making the next eight hours filled with shivers, coughing, and achiness. Our team had to sit around for two hours while Coach Jones attended the wild card meeting. When the coaches emerged, their four choices were a bit surprising. Rittenburg, the wrestler I had just defeated, was awarded one spot, despite losing to two different wrestlers in the same tournament. Ray and I were discussing the decision when Martini chimed in, "Well it makes sense, he lost to Bonora, and since there was no way anyone was beating Bonora, he kind of won the tournament." I just laughed and thanked him. That sentiment, and what my former coach, Mr. Chern once said about cloning my DNA, were probably just offhand remarks long forgotten by those who uttered them, but never by me.

The drive home was long, uncomfortable, and freezing cold. Ray and I did not make it back to our house until 4:00 A.M. The whole ride I was day-dreaming about a hot shower. That moment, when I finally found the water covering my entire body was blissful. I stayed in the shower for more than twenty minutes, letting the water engulf me. When I got out, I fell on my bed, towel and all, and succumbed to exhaustion. I was drained emotionally as much as physically. The rest of my team went out and celebrated. I slept.

Everyone's season officially ended that weekend, except for Martini and me. Six of our teammates were recruited to practice with us until we left for Iowa. The amount of support Martini and I received over those two weeks was tremendous. Ray, Hoyt, Drappi, Sutherland, Guarino, Casey, and Logan came to every practice to push us just a bit more. They were all still floating from our New England title. If Martini and I had only each other to wrestle live with, it would not have been as productive of a training period. We would have gotten too accustomed to the other's moves, and also found it easier to allow ourselves to progressively slack off as our bodies tired. Instead, having a fresh guy coming in every minute did not allow that to happen.

As I was working out with Hoyt one day, my knee locked out for the first time since the preseason and was stuck in that familiar position. I dropped to the mat clutching my leg. Hoyt backed away and with panic in his voice asked if I was okay. I told him I just needed to straighten my leg out real quick. As I was about to snap it back into place, our athletic trainer ran onto the mat and yelled at me to stop. She took my leg, massaged it for a few minutes and then slowly extended it. Instead of the violent snap back into place that I was used to, it gently slide back to where it was supposed to be. My knee was a little tender for the rest of practice but I was able to finish the workout.

To this day I still wonder why my knee locked up, right before nationals. Then I did not have time to give it much thought. I knew I could not let it affect the way I wrestled. If my knee locked while out in Iowa, I would simply have to find a way to overcome it.

Another physical challenge I had to deal with was the after-effects of an injury which had first occurred sometime during the previous semester. Martini and I were having one of our intense scrapping sessions, when he hit me with a blast double to the center of my chest. I folded up like an accordion. From that moment on, every time I fully exerted myself during a live wrestling situation, my chest would scream in agony. The deeply bruised chest plate spelled trouble during a closely contested match. I took comfort in the knowledge that almost everyone at nationals was going to be a bit banged up too. I decided to ignore it as much as I could and treat it in my conventional stubborn way -- by praying.

Despite my chest pain, knee scare, and razor sharp focus, I enjoyed those last practices immensely.

I had been the number one ranked Division III wrestler in the country from the beginning of the season to this point. With my New England performance, I was sure to be the top seed in the national tournament and because of this, I started to receive extra attention. First, an ABC-TV camera crew arrived to interview Martini, Coach Jones, and me. The focus of the story centered on our team's New England championship, the first for our school in sixteen years.

A few days later, I received a phone call from an NCAA reporter, Amy Farnum-Novin. She wanted to write a feature article about me. She explained her reasoning for choosing me, "I picked you since you are not from a Wartburg or Augsburg type school."

I smiled and said, "Isn't that the truth."

Those teams had finished one and two in thirteen consecutive NCAA Division III Wrestling Championships. RIC had never finished in the top ten.

During the phone interview Amy asked, "What will be the key for you to win out in Iowa?"

"I just need to keep my composure," I replied. "If I am faced with a situation where I make a mistake, I have to realize there is enough time in the match to come back…"

I fully believed in my ability, in any situation.

I also did two other phone interviews, one with The Rhode Island Sports Review and the other for my hometown newspaper, The Nutley Journal. When the media coverage subsided, my housemates joked, "Look at our big star."

Traditionally, wrestlers do not wrestle to be in the limelight. I certainly was not a sports star. While I appreciated the attention, I never gave it much thought. My mindset was that when all was said and done, the only thing that would matter was how I felt about everything. If those interviews had not happened, the national tournament would still have been just as significant to me. I trained for years for this shot and now, with two weeks left, I was getting some recognition. That was not what I had pushed myself so hard and worked so many years for.

Right before we were set to ship out, I received two more notes in addition to Robbie's letter which still said, "Do Not Open Until Iowa." Coach Chern wrote me an email, which in his unique way, said exactly what I needed to hear, at the exact moment I needed to hear it. Christina mailed a package of treats and a big card. Her words of encouragement were exactly what I needed to hear. I was now ready to face the biggest challenge of my life.

What You Can Take Away from Chapter 11:

1. Always stay positive.

2. Limit your superstitions to achieve peace of mind.

3. Great wrestlers never attempt to keep the score close, they wrestle to win.

12

CEDAR RAPIDS

Coach Jones, Martini, and I flew to Cedar Rapids, Iowa on Wednesday morning, March 5, 2008. As we neared our hotel room, I noticed the number on the door read '717' (I was born on 7/17). For a split second I thought, "I am going to win this thing." I quickly regrouped and told myself there was a lot of work to be done.

Signs were something I always looked for. It made me smile if I glanced down at the time when it was 1:41, or if a song time on my ipod read 1:41. To see my birth date was a good thing too. I never looked deeply into this. It was just something I had done with all my weight classes since high school. Maybe it was the one superstition I could not shake. Or maybe Ray is right and I am just a crazy lunatic.

Our first practice of the trip was scheduled for Wednesday afternoon. An advantage over the previous season was that I had Martini to wrestle with. During the practice, we thought other wrestlers were scouting us so neither one of us drilled our best moves. Thinking back, I realize we may have just been paranoid that weekend.

In every live situation, (we decided situation wrestling was harder to scout than straight up live wrestling) Martini beat me. It did not matter if I started with his leg in the air or he started with mine, he scored every time. At first this weighed heavily on my mind. I soon changed my thought process and decided, "Good, Martini is ready for this tournament." Thinking that way did not hurt my psyche one bit.

Following our workout, I did a bit more on my own. It was not because I was overweight (the flu had taken care of that), but because I simply wanted to. When I got into my stance, I felt as if I was on the cusp of a great confrontation. I was excited to have the chance to wrestle on one of the eight mats in the awesome facility that was the U.S. Cellular Center and to have a chance at becoming a national champion. A burst of energy flowed through my body. I decided to run ten sprints. It was not enough. I picked up my jump rope and started to sprint while simultaneously jumping rope. Once I had burned off the extra energy, I sat down, stretched and tried to soak it all in. I knew this was my moment to shine. I could not let it slip by. I thought, "I will never be here again." There was only one problem, it was Wednesday and the tournament did not start until Friday.

Since we had over thirty-six hours before weigh-ins, and Martini and I were light, we went out to dinner. Both of us ordered grilled chicken and steamed vegetables with a glass of ice water. I always drank a decent amount of water, two days before a weigh-in.

Martini kept the mood light all day. He constantly cracked me up with random funny lines. The laughter produced a good environment to keep us relaxed and loose two days before the tournament began.

Thursday afternoon our families and friends arrived. It was great to have so much support, since I felt all of Iowa would be against me.

Martini and I greeted our families and friends and then we relaxed. A few hours later when we checked our weights, we learned we only had to lose around two pounds each. At our second workout of the day, both of us lost three pounds in order to eat a peanut butter and jelly sandwich and drink a bottle of water. Then, we started to go through our own pretournament rituals.

Almost every wrestler has these to some extent. Mine centered around food. I had to have everything ready for the moment after weigh-ins the following morning. All that I ate from Thursday until after the tournament was a mixture of granola, walnut, almond, and dried mango, peanut butter and jelly sandwiches on whole wheat bread, oranges, and bananas. Besides food, I liked to have a fresh pair of clothes and a clean singlet for every match. With the bag packed, the challenge of falling asleep began. What I have found out since is that, ironically, trying to stay awake helps me fall asleep. I wish I knew that then. I battled with my thoughts for more than an hour before sleep overtook me.

On Friday morning I woke with nervous energy filling my mind, body, and spirit. My aim was to harness that and use it to my advantage. Martini and I made the walk to the arena a half hour before weigh-ins were set to begin. In the intervening time we joked around and tried to stay calm. The first matches would not start for almost three hours. When our respective weights were made, I ate my preselected foods as if it was any other tournament. Then I relaxed for half an hour before changing into my singlet.

Next on my agenda was warming up to the point of a slight sweat. Watching the facility slowly fill with fans excited me even more. My blood was pumping fast when I heard the arena announcer say, "Will everyone please stand." I assumed the national anthem would follow. Tragically, I was incorrect.

She announced that Scott Viera had passed away and my heart went out to him. He was a RIC graduate, a Roger Williams University assistant coach, and a man I respected. He was always kind and encouraging to all wrestlers. My mind raced back to the conference championships and I was glad I had gone over to him to say hello. During that interaction he told me he was thankful that I sought him out and apologized about not being able to make the trip to Iowa. He had a look which, for anyone who has known someone who died of cancer, was instantly recognizable. When I heard the announcement in Iowa, I said to him softly, "Well now you can be here." Then I ran to the warm-up area and tried to block it all out. I would be wrestling in a half hour and had to get my head clear.

While warming up for the second time before the opening round, many things ran through my mind. In an attempt to stay positive, I focused on myself and smiled that I was flu-free. The two question marks that remained were how my knee and chest would hold up. I could only pray. In the moments before any match, I tended to get pretty tense and this one was no exception. To calm down, I repeated in my head, "I'm the best here, I can do this." It was a cheap way of giving myself a final confidence boost. Confidence is the key to success, as long as it does not spill over into cockiness. By the time the referee blew his whistle to signal the start of the match against my first opponent, I was ready. The moment I heard that sound, my nervousness vaporized, just as it had in all my previous bouts.

When the 2008 NCAA Division III championships began, I could sense my opponent from the University of Wisconsin-Steven's Point, anxiousness wrestling on his feet. I scored on a fireman's carry right away. It was nice to be correct in my hypothesis that in Iowa, the wrestlers would not run from me. The first period ended with a 6-1 score in my favor. Then, the match took a hard turn in the other direction.

It was his choice in the second and he opted for top. It was a smart decision on his part. I was in control from our feet and turned him when I had the top position. For some reason, that simple choice freaked me out. I was not thinking clearly, went into defensive mode and got ridden out the entire second period. For the final period, I optioned back to neutral. The choice proved to be a good one when I added to my lead with another takedown. Almost instantaneously, my lackluster riding ability allowed him to escape. Once back on our feet we were in my domain. Instead of attacking and going for a major decision, I stayed away. This proved to be a terrible strategy, as he scored his first takedown of the match and rode me out until time expired. I was even hit with stalling *twice.*

On the strength of the opening period, I won 8-5. It was not the impressive first round domination I was hoping for. One of the New England coaches told me after, "Mike, you've got to get out on bottom if you want to win this thing." I agreed with him, and then I dropped the match from my thoughts and started to think about my quarterfinals opponent. Dwelling on mistakes would do me no good now.

In the first round, Martini was wrestling an opponent who had beaten him earlier in the season by two points. When this second go-around had thirty seconds left, Martini was in that familiar predicament of being down by a couple of points. Martini did what champions do, and went for it. A scramble ensued where Martini almost brought his opponent to his back. His Loras College counterpart was too strong and reversed him to score five points.

Following Martini's bout I returned to our hotel room and showered, as I tried to do after every match. As Coach Smith used to say about a shower, "It wakes up your nerves." I threw on some comfortable clothes and had a brief conversation with my family. Although for the most part, I kept to myself. It was imperative to stay focused. A little distraction is good, but too much can be counterproductive. I took a nap, since there were five hours between my first and second matches.

I made sure I woke up a full two hours before the quarterfinals showdown. Once awake, it was time to refuel. I ate some mango mixture, drank water, and read the letters from Coach Chern, Robbie, and Christina. Then I got a text message from Coach Chern, "Don't overlook Grawin."

Travis Grawin was the only other returning All-American in the weight class, wrestling for Luther College in Iowa. He had suffered some bad defeats throughout the year. For that reason, his seed had dropped from two to eight. Regardless, it was odd that we had to wrestle each other in the quarters. We were the only two proven wrestlers with All-American plaques hanging on our walls.

I told myself, "It sucks for him that he has to wrestle me now because I have to beat everyone. The order doesn't matter."

Before the match was set to begin, Coach Jones said something that made a lot of sense, "Build an early lead and don't let him have a chance to make a comeback. He has a lot of fans here and you have to make sure they have nothing to cheer about." Going into a match against an Iowa wrestler in his home state was not something I relished. A home field advantage can be huge. Ray slapped my hand prior to stepping on the mat and screamed, "Don't just beat him, kill'im." That was exactly what I set out to do.

At the onset I executed a fireman's carry for four points. The first period ended in the identical 6-1 score of my morning match. Instead of learning from my mistake however, I shut down and tried to protect the lead. Once again, this was not a good plan, nor is it ever. It allowed Grawin a chance to breathe, when I should have smothered him with an onslaught of attacks. Maybe it was a hangover from my plan at the conference championships, who knows?

In the second period, Grawin took me down and I heard chants from the crowd of, "Let's go Travis," ringing loudly in my ears. Taking my foot off the gas pedal did not come back to bite me in the last round, but in this contest, I was on the ropes. Towards the end of a seesaw battle, I found myself up by two points with twenty seconds left. This time, learning from the past, I grabbed a two-on-one, Russian armbar. The referee hit me with stalling for the second time anyway. It cut my lead to one with ten seconds left. At the time I thought, "What the hell did he call that for?" Foolishly, I shot a double leg takedown out of spite and fortunately finished it as time expired to win, 11-8. The takedown in the closing seconds of that match was one of the only times in my career I scored off a double leg.

In my first two matches at nationals, I was called for stalling four times, while in my previous forty-plus matches I had zero stalling calls. Even if I did not agree with the call, I unwisely let a referee be in a position to decide the outcome of the match, when I should have widened the gap between myself and my opponent. As in the first round, my win was not pretty. Nevertheless the match was over and it was time to move on. As part of putting the bout behind me, I thought of Yogi Berra's quote, "It's déjà vu all over again." A year before I had been in the same spot -- the national semifinals.

While walking towards my family after the Grawin match I thought, "Well I'm an All-American again, that's good I guess." A spot in the semis, guaranteed a top six finish in the tournament. Almost as soon as the thought entered my mind, I understood it was not okay for *me*. If I stopped there, I would have been disappointed. A national title was the only thing, at that point, that would have allowed me to leave the sport with my head up.

The next step in my journey was to shed the weight I had added throughout the day. The damage added up to two pounds even with the one pound allowance for consecutive weigh-ins. I threw on a lot of clothes and started the process all wrestlers hate, cutting weight. Since Martini was about to wrestle his second match, I jumped rope while cheering him on.

Unfortunately, he was beaten by his Delaware Valley opponent and became a spectator.

I worked out for another half hour. It was the easiest weight-cutting of my career. I constantly told myself, "This is the last time you will ever have to do this." I repeated three words I heard from champion boxer, Floyd Mayweather Jr. during one of his TV appearances, "Dedication, hard work."

Four pounds of fluids came out of my body with no problem. That meant an extensive meal was coming my way. It consisted of two bottles of water and a peanut butter and jelly sandwich.

The physical aspect of the day was over, yet there was still work to be done. As Sun Tzu wrote in *The Art of War*, "If you know the enemy and know yourself, you need not fear..." Coach Jones had film on my semifinals opponent, Steve Hult from New York University, and I watched it that Friday night. The tape confirmed what I already knew; my adversary was a very good defensive wrestler and brutal from the top position.

The game plan for the semis was to attack him until he could not breathe. I was confident in my ability to score takedowns, it would just take time.

The semifinals had caused me much heartache in the past. The best wrestling in any tournament usually occurs in that round. Once in the finals, the pressure mounts and wrestlers tend to compete cautiously, which sometimes makes for a boring conclusion. The entire 2007-2008 season, I had successfully combated my semifinals demons. Now, on this grand stage, last years' failure was an unwelcomed memory. What I needed was reassurance and I re-read the notes I received prior to nationals to get it.

Reading the letters for the tenth time, I realized how loved I was. A lot people tried to help me win and I was lucky to have such wonderful people in my life.

I then located the sheet that Coach Jones had composed with the wrestlers in my weight class. I crossed-off all of the quarterfinals losers. There were only four names left that night: mine and Hult's, as well as the other semifinalists, Niles Mercer and Jason Adams. Before getting in bed, I packed my bag for one match. The winners of the semis had a long wait until the finals.

One hundred and sixty wrestlers qualified for the 2008 NCAA Division III Wrestling Championships. Half of those wrestlers make it to the second day to earn All-American honors, while the others lose two matches that first day and are eliminated. This sets up potential problems. Once a wrestler's season is over, he wants to let loose and party, understandable after over five months of hard work. The problem was that too many now-eliminated wrestlers clustered together to party on one of the upper floors in the hotel I was staying. When a drunken wrestler decided to do pull-ups on the sprinkler system at 3:30 A.M. the pipe snapped, setting off the fire alarms throughout the hotel.

I was awakened by the most annoying buzzing noise combined with an irritating automated voice demanding evacuation of the building. I thought I was dreaming. This could not be happening the night before the biggest matches of my life. Unfortunately I was not dreaming. The point was driven home when my brother Steve knocked on my door. He had come to help get everything I needed out of the room. I packed my bag and unhappily wandered down eight flights of stairs to wait in a hallway until the alarm stopped. It was too cold to go outside and I was very tired.

For thirty minutes I sat on the concrete floor along with drunken wrestlers, before the alarm ceased. I told myself it was going to be okay and nothing was going to stop me from winning. I took it as another barrier to break through. Back in my room, I stripped down and got into bed. Then, I heard it *again*, "May I have your attention please, may I have your attention please, this is a fire emergency, please evacuate the building." This time, when my mom knocked on the door, I lost my cool, "Screw it, I'm staying in bed. If it's a real fire, call me." After years of working for this chance, I was being robbed of sleep on the eve of my final showdown.

The whole ordeal had taken over an hour and I did not get back to sleep for another hour beyond that. While lying in bed, I thought about how nothing had ever been easy in my career, so why should the final matches be any different? That worked to a point. What really restored my confidence was the thought that my semifinals opponent was also staying in the same hotel. To this day I do not know if that was technically true, but the idea calmed me down. I fell back to sleep at 5:30 A.M. with the same goal I had all along, winning a championship. "I would have won if that damn fire alarm didn't go off," would not be an excuse.

When I woke up on Saturday morning, I tried as best as I could not to think about the overnight debacle. I glanced at my planner, and saw what I had written on my calendar months before in the March 8 spot: "Wake up nothing, go to bed a national champion." That was the plan and I was sticking to it.

It was time.

I woke up light so I drank a bottle of water and ate a peanut butter and jelly sandwich before weigh-ins, refueling as early as possible. On the second day of nationals instead of getting two hours of recovery time after weigh-ins, we would get only one.

In the hour before the match, my thoughts traveled back in time. Steve Hult was a name I knew from my high school days and when I saw that he had come back to wrestling, I figured our paths would eventually cross. Hult was going to be my make-or-break moment and I knew it.

As the match was set to begin and the foam mats compressed beneath my feet, I thought, "Here I am again. Relax and wrestle. This is where dedication and hard work will pay off."

The whistle sounded and I went on the offensive. In my previous two matches, I tanked in the second and third periods. I was determined not to let that happen again. As soon as we clinched, I felt his strength and knew my fireman's carry would not be effective. I turned to my speed, the dart single. On three occasions the shot looked promising, but each time his defense proved too strong. He tied me up and we had stalemate after stalemate. Since Hult did not take a shot in the first period, he was hit with a stall call. His way to take wresters down was off his defense. As the first period drew to a close I had Hult on his butt. He countered by locking through my legs. Team RIC thought we had the two. The referees did not. That call can go either way and in this instance, it went in my opponent's favor. At the end of the first, the score stood, 0-0.

We moved to the second with the choice falling to Hult, who deferred the starting position for choice in the third. Before I even looked to my corner for my coaches' advice, I decided to choose bottom. The game plan going in had been to choose neutral, though when that was formulated, I figured at decision time I would be winning. Now with a tie I had to adapt to the situation and get the first point. Ray, who was coaching me along with Jones, had similar notions and when I pointed down, he screamed, "You better get up then." Coach Jones was completely against this, however; the ultimate choice was mine.

Hult, rode me out the entire two minute period as Ray's words fell by the wayside, and for a split second, I thought of Yogi again.

At the end of the second period, the score was still 0-0, although Hult had accumulated a full two minutes of riding time. In essence, he was leading, 1-0. My riding ability was inadequate in comparison. We were mirroring the match I had with Keith Sulzer at Midlands in December. At the end of the second period of that match the score was 2-2, and Sulzer had also had a riding point firmly in his possession. Before the final period with Sulzer, my mindset had been to let him up and attempt to take him down at the end, ride him out and force overtime. That approach had not worked.

In national semifinals against Hult I was in that elusive, "zone," where thoughts give way to actions. I coached myself in my head, "Let him up and take him down twice to win this match. This is it, this is your moment." There was not another option. I *had* to do it. Then I held up my hands in a diamond shape. It signaled to the referee I was going to let my opponent up and give him a point. Sometimes a step back is the only way forward.

I was consumed with the idea of scoring a takedown. Hult continued in his defensive style and was banged with stalling again. The second stall call earned me a point, making it 2-1, Hult. At that juncture, his riding point could not be erased.

I continued with an offensive attack, took a shot that Hult was apparently ready for, and found myself trapped in a front headlock. That was exactly where I did not want to be. Hult grabbed my foot and pulled down, forcing my knee in the opposite direction of the natural bend. Fortunately, it did not lock my knee out. The referee stopped the match due to the potentially dangerous position. If the referee had not made that call, it would have been over. Hult was definitely going to score and despite the potential danger, another official might not have made the same decision. Regardless of how hard one trains, how prepared one is, the fates may sometimes have different ideas. In this instance, they were on my side.

At the start of the next whistle, I was on Hult quickly. A miniature scramble ensued, ending with me controlling a front headlock. Right away I went for my go-behind-drag, got there, threw my reverse leg in and locked up a merkle position. It was the exact spot Andrew Lacroix and I were in at the 2006 Springfield tournament. Unconsciously, I remembered what the referee had told me then and locked Hult's head and arm between my hands. As soon as the merkle was secured, the two points were mine. When the whistle blew signaling that we were out of bounds, the clock read 0:44.

At this point, I was faced with another decision. If I could ride him out for the remaining time, I would win. The main area I focused on improving over the past two seasons had been my riding ability, and in that time, I had made tremendous progress. Yet, in this situation, to attempt to ride him out did not enter my mind. If I had gotten reversed, Hult would have been heading to the national finals. The plan was to cut him loose and take him down again to win. If he was going to beat me, I wanted it to be in my best position. The choice gave me essentially forty-four seconds to score the two. If not, I would have another minute of overtime. A tied match was fine with me, I had prepared for that. It all added up to me making that diamond shape again.

Now the score was 3-3.

I took a few more shot attempts and found myself in the now-familiar front headlock position with Hult in control again. Not wanting a repeat of the last potentially dangerous situation, I went for the arm drag Florian had taught me five years earlier. It was executed with most of our bodies out of bounds, save for Hult's pinky finger, which was still in. Moments later, as the final seconds ticked away, I was awarded the two points.

The win was easily the biggest of my career. On the walk back to my corner, I held up a finger and repeated, "One more." Coach Jones was overjoyed and said the line back to me, picking me up in a hug. Ray received an emphatic hand slap.

I was in the national finals.

I thought, "Now, I cannot finish any worse than second in the country." Promptly, I dismissed the thought and reminded myself why I was there, "No Mike, it's one or nothing." I had come this far and I was not about to settle.

The other 141 pound semifinals between Adams and Mercer was concluding. To my surprise, Jason Adams from Augsburg College in Minnesota emerged as my finals foe.

Once I knew who was to be my opponent, I wanted to greet my family and Coach Lore. There were tears in their eyes, despite the huge grin on my face. The match had been very nerve racking for them. I hugged everyone, my embrace with Coach Lore unexpectedly the longest. His eyes were almost dried by then and his coaching mind took over. "What were you thinking, choosing bottom against a kid like that?"

My response is lost somewhere in the fabric of time, all I can recall is the joy I felt. What trumped the feeling was that the tournament was not over. I knew I could enjoy my accomplishment for only a few more moments and then I would have to put it behind me.

My family would have more than eight hours to kill before I wrestled my last match. There is always a lot of down time at wrestling tournaments, and while I do not know everything my family did during that time, I do know they were very anxious and felt the pressure too.

The parade of All-Americans was set to start at 6:30 P.M. and it was only 11:30 A.M. I planned to be back in the arena by six. In the time between, I relaxed as best I could. Now, the sheet Coach Jones had made had two more Xs. I decided to give Christina a call and before we hung up, she gave me the same advice she had a year before -- watch a funny movie.

It was a good idea. I needed to take my mind away from wrestling for a bit. I had planned for this situation before leaving Providence, and *As Good as it Gets* with Jack Nicholson was with me in a portable DVD player. That movie always cracked me up and this time it did too. If someone who did not know me walked into that room, they would have never guessed I would be wrestling for a NCAA title a few hours later. When Jack

Nicholson's last joke played, it was still hours before six and I had planned to take a nap. Once again, sleeping and anxiety collided.

Instead, I wandered into Coach Jones's room to talk with Ray and Keith. The topic of conversation turned to what color singlet I was going to wear in the finals. The maroon singlet was my first choice as it would have brought closure to my career, maroon having been my high school color. Then Coach Jones reminded me Augsburg's color was maroon. I thought, "Well I am going for the gold, I might as well wear it." Even though I knew the color of my singlet was not going to affect the outcome of the match, when I went to pack up my bag, I realized, all three of my gold singlets were used.

Sometimes even a graduate student vying for a national championship needs his mom.

At 3:15 I knocked on my parent's door and asked my mom if she could have my singlet cleaned by 5:30. She responded, as I knew she would, "Absolutely Michael. Is there anything else I can do?" She hand-washed it and dried it with a hair dryer. It was ready exactly on time. You cannot beat a mother's love.

In the meantime I ate what seemed like my hundredth peanut butter and jelly sandwich and got back in bed with plans to sleep for an hour. That would give me enough time to pack my bag before I headed down to the arena. Napping was no easier this time. A million thoughts were running through my head and filtering the negative ones out became a nuisance. My mind continually wavered back and forth until I somehow dozed off.

A few minutes later I was awakened by a recognizable noise, followed by, "May I have your attention please, may I have your attention please, this is a fire emergency please evacuate the building." What could I do other than laugh? This time the hotel was only resetting their system. Falling back to sleep was out of the question though. I was off my feet and was as rested as I could be without sleeping. That brought me some peace of mind, though my nerves were making my feet and hands quite clammy.

Minutes before six, I decided to reread the letters from Robbie, Christina, and Coach Chern for the last time. Their absences saddened me. Then again, I knew that if they were there, I would not have had those notes to read. That cheered me up.

It was time to enter the U.S. Cellular Center, by myself, and get mentally prepared.

On the walk into the arena I was amazed to see the finals mat raised on a platform. "This is no joke," ran through my head. I had been in the facility hours earlier and a lot had happened since then. All the bouts were finished except for the finals in each of the ten weight classes. I learned Hult beat Grawin, my quarterfinals opponent, in the third place match. Now I knew that if I won the finals against Adams, I would have beaten the number two, three, and four wrestlers in the country in consecutive matches. There were only seven minutes of work separating me from that storybook ending.

Getting dressed for the last competitive match of my career had the potential to be mentally draining. Not to let my emotions get the best of me, I concentrated on the little things more than ever. I made sure there were no wrinkles in my socks by pulling them up slowly. I slipped into my gold singlet, shorts, and the long sleeve shirt from former teammate Sean Miele. I strapped headgear to the shoulder strap of my singlet and pulled Brian Hoyt's kneepad onto my right leg. Finally, I started the process of putting on Colin Smith's shoes. I thought of many instances where I heard the term, "Lacing them up for the last time." As I pulled my laces tightly, I understood I was not only wrestling for a national championship, I was wrestling my final match.

Once dressed, I lined up with the seventy-nine other All-Americans for the parade. The ceremony could not have been over quickly enough. Never in my life had I been more ready to wrestle. At the same time I remembered the year before when I had been envious of the finalists. Now my mind was not on how lucky I was to be in the finals, only on how to win.

With the conclusion of the ceremony, the non-finalists dispersed to their seats to watch, and the finalists warmed up. It was there where I made my last energy packet. Having the flu during the conference championships encouraged me to use them, and at nationals I was simply continuing the trend I had set two weeks prior. As soon as I took one sip, the cup slipped out of my hand and spilt onto the floor. I laughed and thought, "Guess someone up there thinks it's a bad idea to drink that." Earlier in my career, something as simple as that could have rattled me. This time, I simply reassured myself that the packet was not the reason why I had won.

I took part in a drilling session with the defending 133 pound national champion, Dave Morgan from King's College in Pennsylvania. When we were done, I had a lot of nervous energy left so I ran a few sprints to calm down.

There was a loud cheer as Seth Flodeen from Augsburg won the 125 pound national title via the pin. Augsburg had plenty of fans who had made the drive from Minnesota. When it was Morgan's turn, he won in overtime against his opponent from Wartburg College.

Then, it was *my* time.

Coach Jones and Ray escorted me to the holding area opposite of Adams. When the announcer called my name, I ran up the stairs and onto the mat. The feeling was incomparable and energized me even more. Anytime a bad thought entered my mind, I did what had been working all weekend -- countered the negative with a positive.

While stripping down to my singlet, Coach Jones and Ray arrived in my corner. On my way to the center of the blue mat for the pre-match handshake, I took a look around and thought, "Wow."

The final match of the 141 pound weight class that season began as every other one, with a whistle. In contrast to the national semifinals, I felt stronger than Adams during our first clinch. Due to the slight edge in strength I assumed my fireman's carry would be effective. Unfortunately for me, Augsburg had coached their wrestler well. Every time I set up for the move, Adams threw a wrench into my well-oiled takedown machine. Without adapting to my new situation as I had done with Hult, throughout this match, I repeatedly went for the fireman's.

When prepping for the championships, relying solely on that shot was something I tried to avoid. Nevertheless, I succumbed to the common finals' tendency and wrestled too cautiously.

Cautious wrestling is not always ill-advised. One good shot attempt that results in a takedown is definitely better than ten that do not, and if Adams had scored the first points, my strategy would have undoubtedly changed. The plan with no score was to capitalize off his mistakes. Adams opened the door for me on his first shot attempt. His body movement right before the explosion tipped me off. I countered by tossing him. Recognizing his mistake immediately, Adams recovered in time to roll through back to his feet for no points.

I had let a major opportunity slip through my fingers.

Following the throw, and the shouts of "wow" from the crowd, the excitement waned until there were just thirty seconds left in the first period. Adams took another shot which I countered with a front headlock. This was the position I wanted to be in. I attempted my go-behind-drag and spun behind him. He would not concede the points and countered with a roll. Anticipating this, I caught him on his back. He was flat for two seconds. In those two brief seconds, I was elated, thinking the national title was mine. By the time the official circled around us, Adams had rolled through to his stomach. I had the two points for the takedown and nothing more.

The match would continue.

The instant we rolled through, I stopped thinking about what could have been and planned my next attack. I finished the period in the top position with a two point lead.

Adams deferred the choice in the second period to me. Immediately after my semifinals performance, Coach Jones had made me promise to choose neutral when this time came. If the finals match was scoreless as in the semis at this juncture, I would have made the same decision as I did then and chosen to go down, despite my coach's pleadings. While I still think I could have gotten out, since I had a lead in the finals, I chose the neutral position and conceded the point.

The whistle blew to start the second period. We had a minor scuffle where I threw my reverse leg in and locked up his head and arm for two more points. Right after the referee awarded the takedown, Adams high legged over and grabbed my leg. We struggled for around thirty seconds until we were out of bounds. I had no control. The official granted Adams an escape to make the score 4-1. However, the whole time I was fighting his reversal attempt, I was building riding time. When we were signaled out of bounds, I had amassed a 1:01 advantage. If nothing else changed, I would get a point for riding and win by a score of 5-1.

With about ten seconds left in the second period, Adams surprised me with a slick shot and got my leg in the air with ease. I went for a counter that had served me well in the past, the knee slip, and that allowed me to wiggle out. It is not a move that I was ever taught, just something I did naturally. Adams was unaware of how to counteract my counter and the second period ended at 4-1.

The 2008, 141 pound national championship now moved into its final stage. The referee pointed to my opponent indicating it was his choice in the last period. Wisely for him, he chose down and escaped in less than ten seconds. I failed to tighten the grip on the riding point. The miscue on my part made the score, 4-2 with 1:53 left. If he took me down and rode me for nine seconds, he would force overtime.

That possibility made me wrestle even more cautiously than I had in the opening. Unlike then when I was waiting for him to make a mistake, in this instance it was to ensure that I did not falter. My objective at that point was to hold on. Trying to hold on at the end of matches is an ill-advised strategy; this was another instance at nationals where I did not wrestle to the best of my ability.

As the announcers pointed out in the third period, Adams was challenging. It was no longer a foregone conclusion that my name would be out in front on the championship bracket. For about a minute, I was trapped in a front headlock. Due to my many battles with my former coach Florian, I was comfortable in the position. In the back of my mind, the scare with Hult also lingered.

What I should have done was drag out to score two more points, sealing the match. What I did was hold onto Adam's elbow with all my might, keeping my head below the center of his chest. As long as my head was there, he could not score. He made many unsuccessful attempts to tap my knee, spin behind and grab my ankle. In the closing moments his grip loosened and the position was reversed. Once in control, I squeezed him as tight as my arms allowed me to.

When the final buzzer sounded with a 5-2 score in my favor, the first thing I did was point to my family, then to the New England section. When my arm was raised triumphantly, I felt what Malcolm X wrote, "I experienced a tingling up my spine as I've never had before or since…"

I will never forget the sound of the words which followed the buzzer, as a female voice burst through the arena, "The championship goes to the number one spot, Michael Bonora, Rhode Island." I had visualized and dreamed of that moment for so long and now it was here.

The national title was mine.

A few months later when asked, "How did you feel standing in the middle of the mat like that?" I thoughtlessly replied, "Amazing." What I should have said and what I meant was, "Like everything had been worth it." The moment was worth every ounce of sacrifice, pain, sweat, and tears. All of the occasions when my fate had hung by a thread went right out of my head. The joy I felt was ninety percent happiness and ten percent relief. This was the exact opposite of every other win of my entire career. Pride filled my body as it hit me: I did exactly what I set out to do. It was my moment. I was fulfilled.

The rest rushed by in a muted blur. The Iowa referee congratulated me. I saw my two aunts in the stands and pointed to them. I turned to shake the Augsburg coach's hand, but he was already walking down the platform, so I bee-lined to my corner where he congratulated me later. As I jogged towards Ray and Coach Jones, my emotions were off the charts. Our embrace was low-key, a classic wrestler and coaches' clench, but no less meaningful for its simplicity.

A volunteer from Coe College, the school hosting the championships, sought me out and said he had to follow me until the end of the tournament. He was my "shadow." The NCAA tested every titlist for illegal substances and at some point I would have to produce a urine sample. For some reason the thought gave me the creeps. I knew I had not taken steroids or cheated in any other way, but I was just recently sick with the flu and had ingested plenty of cold medicine. Now all I could do was pray that none of it contained anything illegal.

By that time, all I wanted to do was find my family in the stands. My shadow and I were heading up there when I noticed that I did not have my credentials. All wrestlers and coaches had been issued a card to allow them to go wherever they wanted in the arena. I figured that it would not matter as any security guard would recognize I was a competitor. On the way up the stairs however, I was stopped by a woman who asked for my pass. I told her I left it in my bag and was just going up to see my family. "You're not allowed passed me without it," was the response. My shadow said, "He just won a national title, it's pretty clear he's a wrestler." None of our explanations satisfied her and we were stuck in limbo between the first and second levels. I said to myself, "This isn't going to bother me now."

My family came down to meet me on the staircase platform and when the embraces and congratulations subsided, I informed them of the impending drug test. Steve said, "Someone thinks you did steroids, look at you, that's a joke."

It was time to get back down to the floor for my turn on the award stand along with the other seven All-Americans at 141. Waiting in my seat, I had to bite my lip to control my joy.

And then, almost too quickly, I was on top of the podium. A photograph was snapped and I glanced to my left and right and noticed that this time, I stood the highest. This moment was almost as fulfilling as the seconds immediately following the final buzzer. After all the years I had pictured and imagined those experiences, both were everything I had hoped. All the times I told myself to go a little further because one day my hard work would be rewarded, were now validated.

With my trophy and bracket in hand, I sat back down to watch the last matches of the 2008 Division III season. At the same time, my mind was reflecting back on my season and career. I smiled when I thought about how often, as a young boy, I used to wish I was a WWF champion. "It can't be better than this," I told myself. My thoughts then turned towards Christina's letter in which she had written, "Win it for yourself. Everyone is already so proud of you."

The next joy was the champions' photo in which I had longed for many years to be included. At first, my dream might have been satisfied with a New Jersey state champions' photo. When I thought about it, I realized that if I had achieved that goal, perhaps, the 2008 national champions' picture would have a different face in the 141 pound spot.

I was the last wrestler to finish and pass the drug test at 10:00 P.M. Coach Jones and I made our way to a celebratory dinner with my family and friends. A few speeches were made so I decided to make one of my own. I found out then that, despite being a national champion on the wrestling mat, I could add public speaking to a long list of shortcomings. It did not matter. The day was one of the best in my memory bank.

What You Can Take Away from Chapter 12:

1. It is human to be nervous when doing things which are important to you.

2. Your best moves might not work in your biggest matches, you need other options.

3. Bad things happen when you protect the lead.

4. Do not change how you wrestle in the finals.

5. Taking steroids or any other performance-enhancing drugs is cheating, and one way or another it will cost you in the end.

13

YOUR DESTINY

Throughout my career, days turned into weeks, weeks yielded to months, and months morphed to years. The things that remained constant throughout the chaos of life were my goals. With all of the roadblocks, misfortunes, and bad luck, there were many chances to turn back and give up. I could have been content with what I had accomplished before winning nationals. But, I never settled and neither should you. Do what you set out to do and get what you set out to get. Desire and perseverance are what separates the great from the best, the champions from the rest. If I did not win nationals, I would not have been able to say it was because of anything I had neglected to do. I am as proud of that, as I am of winning. The easy way out was never a path I followed. I challenge you not to either.

The best compliment I heard in the weeks that followed Cedar Rapids was "well deserved." Almost everyone who congratulated me attached those two words. My friend, Colin, pointed it out one day and added, "That must be a good feeling." He was right.

On the other hand, deserving and doing are not interchangeable terms. I once thought, five years earlier, that I "deserved" a New Jersey state title. That notion proved meaningless. Therefore what I "deserved" during college, never entered my mind. What really matters is how you perform when the pressure is on. Dedication and hard work will put you in the best possible position to win, but ultimately, it is how you perform during the championship rounds that count. Saying, "I deserve this or that...," will only make you feel sorry for yourself, possibly angry, bitter, and cheated out of something if you do fall short. What you should do is everything in your power to accomplish your goal, and you will not feel slighted, regardless of the outcome.

There are no shortcuts in this sport. If there is only one thing you get out of this book let it be this -- your hard work will pay off. I promise you that. It just may not be when, what, or how you thought.

One of the best goals you can have is for your ambition to far exceed your talent. Take yourself further than your God-given ability allows. Think about what scenario you would be more proud of: If you were born the most gifted wrestler in the country, worked out like the average person, and rode your talent to a national championship. Or, you were born with average talent, trained harder and smarter than any person you ever met, and then, propelled by your work ethic, won that same national title.

The first option is too easy and wrestling is never easy. The second scenario is my story, and the long, hard journey made the conclusion even more satisfying. Now *you* have to find *your* place at the top of the podium. It may not be a wrestling championship, it may not even be in sports, but it is my guess you will get there because of the principles you learned as a wrestler.

I have come a long way from the backup wrestler I once was in high school. I wish you my kind of success, on the mat and off it. Now, go after your dreams and understand that *you* are the driving force of *your destiny*. Wrestling is years of pain for

WRESTLING WITH YOUR DESTINY

moments of glory. Through wrestling there are many paths to greatness. You may have to cut down the trees, pave the road, and then sprint toward your goal. Your path might not be one well traveled, but that is what makes it interesting, rewarding, and fulfilling. Enjoy your journey.

APPENDIX A

A DAY IN THE LIFE

I want to describe what an average day in my life was as a college wrestler. It will give you an idea as to whether or not you want to make that gigantic commitment. However, the title of this appendix is a bit misleading. While many days are similar, almost never are they exactly the same. A match day is different than the day before, as a day in October is different from a day in March.

The most fundamental aspect for college athletes is time management. Sports, specifically wrestling, take up vast amounts of time. You could easily get lost in the web that is wrestling and have no time for anything else. Living on your own for the first time can turn into a disaster without a plan to succeed. I recommend keeping a detailed calendar or planner, in which you list everything that you have to do each day. That way you can balance the most important aspects of your life including academics, athletics, and social.

Many athletes and students succumb to the temptations of constant partying in their first year of college. Nothing proactive can get accomplished in that scenario with respect to grades and particularly athletics. Most institutions require freshmen members of sports' teams to attend an organized study hall for a few hours each week. At RIC, if a student-athlete's GPA was over a 2.5 in the first semester, they were no longer required to attend. It was a good system that forced me to put time into the most important part of a college career, which is academics. While I hated the idea at the time, it turned out to be very beneficial for both my grades and for wrestling too. Remember you are a student-athlete, not an athlete-student. Setting aside six hours a week for school work is a plan you should put in place for yourself, even if your institution does not.

Here is how I typically divided up the time spent in various activities.

Arguably, the most vital part of the day is the eight hours of sleep an athlete needs. Practice ran about two and a half hours daily, and was normally preceded and/or followed by one to two hours of workout time on my own, totaling about, four hours of training per day. During our school's winter break, we had double sessions, and trained five to six hours a day. The typical student-athlete has three hours of class time each day. Combined with sleep and training, that accounts for fifteen of the twenty-four hours. As a senior in my house I spent at least an hour preparing my food and then another eating it. When you are a freshman, chances are you will have a meal plan through your college but the time spent in the cafeteria will be comparable to living on your own. During winter break when I remained on campus to train, I would also take a nap, watch a movie, or read for two to three hours. However, when classes were being conducted I would spend those hours doing homework. This leaves only four or five hours which I spent on the phone (with my girlfriend mostly), on the computer, and relaxing with friends.

My days during wrestling season were not exactly fun in the sense that I was not doing what many other college students do, i.e. getting drunk and/or high and staying up all hours of the night partying. I chose a different path; in my opinion, a better one. Those typical fun college times are usually forgotten in the blur of what is the college experience. My time in college was not littered with alcohol and drugs, but with hard work, dedication, determination, and sacrifice. I am very grateful for that.

During my freshman season at Rhode Island, on two occasions, I made the mistake of getting drunk. I cannot remember one thing about either of those nights now. Yet I know *I will never forget* the feelings of anguish after my season ended. Had I let getting drunk become a habit, I would not have been able to continue to train properly, compete consistently, and succeed in wrestling.

APPENDIX B

TYING UP LOOSE ENDS

Many of the people I met during my senior season thought everything was easy for me. That could not be further from the truth. For every single year of my career, save the final one, I envied other wrestlers for how simple they made wrestling look. I eventually became that person people looked up to, even though I was not conscious of it at first. It took ten years of hard work to reach that point. I learned that it is always more rewarding when you have to work and wait for something.

Just like everyone else I have many weaknesses. This point was driven home when one of my fellow graduate assistants at RIC asked, "Mike, do you have *any* problems or vices?" She said it in a serious tone with a face free of sarcasm. At the time, I did not realize she was paying me a tremendous compliment. In that moment, I hesitated before replying, "lots." The question helped me grasp that what is important is how we counter our vices and problems, not what they are.

A major problem I had to deal with was the Madelung's deformity in my wrists. The abnormality caused a lot of pain over the years, and made it difficult for me to perform many exercises, such as pushups. I avoided things that hurt my wrists and coped with my problem as best I could. During my sophomore year of high school, a doctor told me never to wrestle again. By that time my love for the sport, or maybe addiction to it, had grown too strong to walk away. Instead, I tackled the problem head on by improving my grip strength.

I was advised on two other occasions not to wrestle because of my back ailments. I have a "Sherman Back" which is a slight hunchback, and a degenerative disk. Because of those problems I am constantly shifting around due to an endless nagging pain. My doctor told me not to lift weights before the 2007-2008 season. I modified the orders to cater to my needs, without putting too much strain on my back.

I am not telling you these things for sympathy, but to help you see that everyone, including champions, have physical, mental, and personal difficulties to overcome. Substitute my problems with your own and then deal with what is on your plate. Remember everyone is human and has to overcome some odds to be great.

Greatness is similar to a good idea, no one thinks it is possible otherwise they would have done it themselves. Think about how many people probably laughed at the guy who said, "Let's bottle water and sell it!" Goals and ideas are similar and you may encounter people who will try to tear yours down.

No matter what your goal is in wrestling, know that it is doable because it has been done before. If you want to be a national champion, keep in mind that every single year one is crowned at your weight class. I always said to myself, "Someone has to win, so why not me?" Whether your goal is winning a state title or an Olympic one, others have already done it. Let that knowledge comfort and empower you.

The quickest and most effective way to become a better wrestler is simply to wrestle. Never waste practice time, especially drilling time. Try to learn one new thing each session. After practice you should be able to say, "This helped me in some way" (besides keeping your weight down). The second you stop improving every day, you stop gaining ground.

Focus on the little things such as where your hands go when your partner is shooting *his* shots. Just because you are playing a dummy when your teammate takes you down, does not mean you have to think like one too.

When you are drilling make sure you shoot the same move three or four times before switching. If you make a mistake on your first shot, it is much easier to correct it a split second later than it would be after your partner went. You want to develop muscle memory. By drilling the same things over and over, your body remembers on its own how to do things. That is why athletes often say, "I don't know what I did, it just happened."

When it comes to actual wrestling you should concern yourself with neutral wrestling first. If you can take someone down you can win a match. For that reason, it is the most important position. Position is the key word in the previous sentence as well as in all of wrestling. Someone with incredible positioning is hard to beat even if they have little else to offer. On your feet you have three lines of defense: head, hands, and hips. Use them all.

Subsequently, focus on getting out from bottom. It enables you to get back to your feet, into what is hopefully your best domain. After you are great from those two spots, then and only then, concern yourself with top wrestling. Any points you can score from there should be looked on as free points. There are rare exceptions to this rule, as there are to all rules.

Technically you should be three moves deep, meaning if your number one move does not work, use your second, then third, if necessary. That philosophy can be applied to all aspects of the sport. On my feet I had my fireman's, dart shot, and a sweep single leg. Sometimes even those were not enough as nationals proved. Transitioning from move to move without stopping to reset will eventually score you points.

I also highly recommend developing a good front headlock. Scoring off your opponent's shots is essential to success. Too many wrestlers simply block their adversaries before letting them back up. Doing that invites them to keep on shooting until they do score. If you have a good front headlock your opponent will think twice about shooting again. You also have to be great at preventing a takedown in the reverse position. I was happy in either spot of the front headlock. This gave me the confidence to shoot as much as I wanted.

There are, of course, other ways to make progress. When lifting for wrestling, target the muscles used the most; legs, forearms, neck, and back. Most importantly, work the hardest where you are the weakest. One of wrestling's many beauties is that hard work can trump talent.

There is a point in the season when wrestlers think that their weight is finally under control. This tends to be the wrestlers who do not lift during the season. The reason for their weight stabilizing is that they lose muscle mass, not fat. That is the exact opposite of what you want. In spite of how tired you are, you have to do maintenance lifting. Any time spent in the weight room is better than none.

The point at which your body can go no more is actually well passed where you think it is. If you are asking yourself whether you should go on a run, whether or not you should do these workouts, *do it*. Before practice, get to the gym and lift. After practice is over, run sprints on your own. If you can think to yourself, "Can I go harder?" you can. If you could not, you would not be able to think. Dan Gable, the most celebrated wrestler in American history, wanted to be carried off the mat when practice was over. That is how hard he worked and he accomplished world and Olympic glory with gold medals in the most prestigious wrestling tournaments.

Read books to help yourself. I read any book that I thought would help me reach my goal, even if it was unrelated to wrestling. Some of the books I chose were *Warrior of the Light* by Paul Coelho, *The Winner Within* by Pat Riley, *Sports Psyching* by Thomas Tutko and Umberto Tosi, *It's Not about the Bike* by Lance Armstrong, *Four Days to Glory* by Mark Kreidler and many others. I picked up a few great pointers along the way.

Be sure to learn about nutrition. There is a plethora of great books and websites on the topic. Many wrestlers handle their weight the wrong way and it negatively affects their performances. Eating the right foods on a match day and in the days leading up to it are essential to competing at your highest level. What worked for me on match days was a small amount of food and a lot of fluids. Find the right mix for your body.

Wrestling is one of the few sports in which you get out exactly what you put in. No matter how much a 5'4" kid practices basketball, the chances of him competing at the highest level are extremely slim. As opposed to a wrestler of any size, who can find himself on the sport's grandest stage.

Remember that while we envy others during the season, non-athletes who spend time eating, drinking, going to parties instead of working out, dieting and getting enough rest, also envy us. Many teenagers and young adults look at their counterparts on sports teams, or really anyone dedicated to achieving an important goal, and wish they had what it takes to make the necessary sacrifices. Enjoy all of the moments. You will never have them again.

The eastern philosopher Mencius said, "It is often through adversity that men acquire virtue, wisdom, skill, and cleverness." Adversity crosses every path traversed by those who accomplish great feats. You have to understand that you will not be 100 percent every match. I can guarantee that Cael Sanderson, the only undefeated four-time NCAA Division I Champion, did not feel his best before all of his matches. What he did do was reach inside and come up with enough to win every time. That is what matters. Whatever situation you find yourself in, if it is your worst day or your best, you have to dig deep to find the strength to win. And you can do it. Remember that: You can do it.